SpringerBriefs in Criminology

AF783318

More information about this series at http://www.springernature.com/series/10159

Celline Cole • Resy Vermeltfoort

U.S. Government Contractors and Human Trafficking

Two Case Studies of Iraq and Bosnia-Herzegovina

Springer

Celline Cole
Heidelberg, Germany

Resy Vermeltfoort
Amsterdam, The Netherlands

ISSN 2192-8533 ISSN 2192-8541 (electronic)
SpringerBriefs in Criminology
ISBN 978-3-319-70826-3 ISBN 978-3-319-70827-0 (eBook)
https://doi.org/10.1007/978-3-319-70827-0

Library of Congress Control Number: 2017959551

© The Author(s) 2018
This work is subject to copyright. All rights are reserved by the Publisher, whether the whole or part of the material is concerned, specifically the rights of translation, reprinting, reuse of illustrations, recitation, broadcasting, reproduction on microfilms or in any other physical way, and transmission or information storage and retrieval, electronic adaptation, computer software, or by similar or dissimilar methodology now known or hereafter developed.
The use of general descriptive names, registered names, trademarks, service marks, etc. in this publication does not imply, even in the absence of a specific statement, that such names are exempt from the relevant protective laws and regulations and therefore free for general use.
The publisher, the authors and the editors are safe to assume that the advice and information in this book are believed to be true and accurate at the date of publication. Neither the publisher nor the authors or the editors give a warranty, express or implied, with respect to the material contained herein or for any errors or omissions that may have been made. The publisher remains neutral with regard to jurisdictional claims in published maps and institutional affiliations.

Printed on acid-free paper

This Springer imprint is published by Springer Nature
The registered company is Springer International Publishing AG
The registered company address is: Gewerbestrasse 11, 6330 Cham, Switzerland

This work was adapted from two theses written and submitted to the Master program International Crimes and Criminology at the Vrije University of Amsterdam (VU).

Celline Cole: From Workers to Victims – Human Trafficking and Forced Labor of Third Country Nationals by U.S. Government Contractor KBR, Inc. in Iraq (2016)

and

Resy Vermeltfoort: From Peacekeepers to Perpetrators – Case Study of Private Contractor DynCorp and Their Complicity in Sex Trafficking in Post-War Bosnia (2015)

Both Master theses were supervised by Prof. Dr. Wim Huisman.

Foreword

Since the Nuremberg trials after World War II, the involvement and complicity of companies in gross human rights violations has been acknowledged. Today, corporations can and do play an important role in the commission of international crimes, by tolerating or supplying the means for the commission of these crimes and supporting the perpetrators of these crimes. Criminal investigations as well as tort lawsuits have been initiated in various countries. However, no corporation has ever been convicted for complicity to international crimes or other gross human rights violations.

Most prevalent in accusations of corporate involvement in gross human rights violations are companies that belong to the extractive industries. Following scholarly debates on the "resource curse" thesis and the "grievance-not-greed" thesis on the convergence of natural resource richness, armed conflict, and gross human rights violation in certain countries, the involvement of the extractive industries should not come as a surprise. Also, the Panel of Experts on the Illegal Exploitation of Natural Resources and Other Forms of Wealth of the Democratic Republic of Congo (DRC), established by the UN Security Council, found that 157 corporations were directly or indirectly involved in illegal exploitation, thus enabling the purchase of arms and the commission of war crimes and crimes against humanity. As such, the DRC case framed the role of corporations in the trade of conflict commodities.

Similarly, the case of Operation Iraqi Freedom framed the harmful role private military and security companies (PMSCs) can play in (post)conflict situations. The risk of companies in particular industries of becoming involved in atrocity crimes is mainly related to the nature of their business (type of product of service, e.g., arms, security) or the place where the business is found (e.g., fragile states, countries of armed conflict or authoritarian rule). This is particularly true for PMSCs. The phenomenon of mercenaries being paid for fighting wars is perhaps as old as warfare itself. The archetype of modern-day PMSCs was Executive Outcomes, founded by former members of the South African Defence Force. Executive Outcomes helped to defeat discredited insurgencies in the 1990s in Angola and Sierra Leone, presenting itself as a stabilizing force for African development.

The use of PMSCs dramatically increased during Operation Iraqi Freedom. Most prevalent for the public image of this new industry was the PMSC Blackwater that came under scrutiny because of numerous violent incidents in which both Iraqi civilians and private contractors were killed. This company was single-handedly responsible for the tarnished reputation the private military industry has suffered ever since. As mentioned by the authors in this book, the involvement in international crimes affects the legitimacy of the (private) military and security industry, including peacekeepers, private contractors, and in some cases even the UN. The two cases presented in this book offer an in-depth analysis of the involvement of two PMSCs in a specific form of human rights abuse: human trafficking.

Part I by Cole aims at revealing the dynamics and explanatory factors behind the crimes of human trafficking and forced labor perpetrated by the American company Kellogg, Brown & Root (KBR) and their subcontractors during Operation Iraqi Freedom and the subsequent U.S. occupation of Iraq. Part I documents how workers deployed by KBR and its subcontractors were frequently being subjected to a wide range of labor abuses that have repeatedly been qualified as forced labor and modern slavery. The case makes clear that the described practices and depicted cases involving KBR and their subcontractors fall under internationally recognized as well as US legal definitions of human trafficking and forced labor. The committed crimes could even be considered crimes against humanity under the provision on enslavement. In Part I, Cole offers an explanation of the involvement of KBR and their subcontractors in human trafficking in Iraq by using the theoretical model of "state-corporate crime."

PMSCs can not only commit international crimes during armed conflict but also be involved in crimes during security and peacekeeping operations after conflict. Part II by Vermeltfoort records such a case of the transformation process of peacekeepers into perpetrators of crimes. At the end of 1995, the brutal war in Bosnia came to an end when the parties to the conflict signed the Dayton Peace Agreement. As part of the United Nations peacekeeping mission in Bosnia and Herzegovina, the private military company DynCorp was assigned to advise and monitor the local Bosnian police, especially on human rights. However, employees of DynCorp became involved in brutal sex trafficking of underage girls. Part II offers an extensive case analysis to explain this transformation process of DynCorp employees from peacekeepers into perpetrators of such human rights abuses. By applying and even adjusting the state-corporate crime model, Vermeltfoort explains how the well-intentioned peacekeeping mission in Bosnia, from both DynCorp and the U.S. government, could turn into involvement in a major sex trafficking scene.

This book adds to the existing literature on state-corporate crime and the involvement of corporations in (gross) human rights violations in a number of ways. First, the two cases discussed in this book illustrate that PMSCs can be involved in human rights abuses beyond the atrocities directly related to armed conflict and that in postconflict situations, PMSCs face other human rights challenges. Second, while the role of the extractive industries and other industries in the commission of international crimes and gross human rights violations in situations of armed conflict and fragile states has already been studied, the human rights impact of the private military and security sector has not yet received much scholarly attention. Third, the book offers the application of the state-corporate crime model to cases outside the context of industrialized and developed countries. In the original framing and application of this model, "state" most referred to the government of the United States. In contexts such as discussed in this book, "state" has a different meaning. It can refer to the host state which in these cases is a weak state being unable to regulate the activities of foreign PMSCs and to the home states of these companies that are unwilling to do so. Fourth, while the cases prove the applicability of the state-corporate crime model for understanding the involvement in human rights abuses, the analysis provided also shows the limits of the model for this purpose. Part II offers a revised analytical framework, taking into account the dynamics between parent company and the subunit level of analysis, increasing the explanatory power of the model for understanding how private contractors of PMSCs become involved in human trafficking or other human rights abuses. As such, the analysis adds new variables and causal mechanisms to the state-corporate crime model.

I applaud Springer for acknowledging the talent of the two young scholars who author this book and for giving them the opportunity to publish their research. The authors belonged to the very best students of the graduate program of criminology and international crimes at VU Amsterdam and have since then worked for international organizations in the field of human rights. Their research offers a valuable contribution to the criminology of state-corporate crime in general and the involvement of PMSCs in human rights abuses in particular. This book is a must-read for any student or scholar interested in corporate crime, postconflict peacekeeping, human trafficking, and the new field of criminology of international crimes and gross human rights violations.

Wim Huisman
Vrije Universiteit Amsterdam
The Netherlands

Acknowledgments

Our sincere thanks go to the people who were indispensable in supporting us in the process of writing our theses and this book: Foremost among those are our supervisor Wim Huisman and our second assessors Willem de Haan and Annika van Baar, who were sincerely interested in the subject matter and provided tremendous insight and guidance in the world of corporate complicity in international crimes. We would like to extend our appreciation to them as our teachers for the course *corporations and international crimes*. Furthermore, Resy Vermeltfoort especially acknowledges Kathryn Bolkovac and Madeleine Rees and thanks them for their time and openness during the interviews for this research. Our deepest gratitude is expressed to all friends and family members who devoted their time to reading and providing feedback on our theses.

Contents

About the Authors

Celline Cole studied psychology, criminology, and international criminal justice in Heidelberg and Amsterdam. She is a 2016 cum laude graduate of the M.Sc. program in international crimes and criminology at Vrije Universiteit (VU) Amsterdam where she also worked as a researcher at the Center for International Criminal Justice (CICJ). Her main research and personal interests are human trafficking, mental health and human rights, and psychosocial interventions in conflict zones. Celline recently completed a four-month internship in the Mental Health Policy and Service Development Team at the World Health Organization (WHO) in Geneva and is currently pursuing a further graduate degree in clinical psychology at Freie Universität Berlin.

Resy Vermeltfoort holds a bachelor's degree in journalism and political science and graduated from the M.Sc. program in international crimes and criminology at the Vrije Universiteit (VU) Amsterdam. She worked as a human rights and advocacy officer at Refugee Law Project, a community outreach project of the School of Law, Makerere University, Uganda. During her time with Refugee Law Project, her thematic areas of focus were transitional justice and gender-based violence against men and boys during conflict. Resy currently works on the topics of gender equality and women's economic empowerment at SNV Netherlands Development Organisation, Vietnam.

Abbreviations

ATCA	Alien Tort Claims Act
BiH	Bosnia and Herzegovina
CPA	Coalition Provisional Authority
CRS	Congressional Research Service
DoD	United States Department of Defense
DoS	United States Department of State
EO	Executive Order
ICC	International Criminal Court
IPTF	International Police Task Force
KBR	Kellogg, Brown & Root
LOGCAP	Logistics Civil Augmentation Program
MEJA	Military Extraterritorial Jurisdiction Act
NGO	Nongovernmental organization
PMC	Private military contractor
PMC	Private military company
PMSC	Private military and security company
POGO	Project on Government Oversight
PSC	Private security contractor
PSV	Police sexual violence
SOFA	Status of force agreement
TCN	Third Country National
TVPA	Trafficking Victims Protection Act
TVPRA	Trafficking Victims Protection Reauthorization Act
UCMJ	Uniform Code of Military Justice
UN	United Nations
UNMBIH	United Nations Mission in Bosnia and Herzegovina
UNO	United Nations Organization
UNSC	United Nations Security Council
US	United States
USG	US Government
VP	Vice President

Part I
From Workers to Victims: Human Trafficking and Forced Labor of Third Country Nationals by U.S. Government Contractor KBR, Inc. in Iraq

Chapter 1
Introduction

Public outrage sparked when in the year 2000 reports began to surface about UN peacekeepers employed by the US private military contractor (PMC) DynCorp being involved in a sex trafficking ring in Bosnia. Numerous organizations dedicated their work to investigating these grave abuses demanding action from the international community as well as from the US Government (USG). Consequently, shortly after the revelation of the crimes perpetrated in Bosnia, the USG publicly committed to combat human trafficking both nationally and internationally, introducing new anti-trafficking laws and regulations. But despite these endeavors, it did not take long for new allegations of human trafficking involving USG contractors to surface and this time on an even larger scale.

In the early 2000s, an increasing number of news stories appeared reporting about cases of human trafficking and forced labor of so-called Third Country Nationals (TCNs) in US-occupied Iraq.[1] TCNs are individuals, predominantly from developing countries like India, Nepal, and Sri Lanka, who are employed on US military bases in Iraq to perform low-wage jobs like construction, cleaning, and food services. TCNs are usually hired by US PMCs who have been put in charge of running the logistics at military bases in Iraq by the USG. These contractors, in turn, regularly employ local subcontractors to recruit personnel for the military bases (ACLU & Yale Law School, 2012).

The overwhelming majority of the reported cases involve the main contractor in Iraq, KBR, Inc. (formerly known as Kellogg, Brown & Root, Inc.; hereafter KBR) and several of the company's subcontractors accusing them of being engaged in human trafficking and several forms of serious labor abuses of TCNs on military bases (Brown, 2007). The accusations involve trafficking of TCNs

[1] USG contractors in Afghanistan have also reportedly engaged in practices of human trafficking and forced labor. However, this thesis will only focus on KBR in Iraq as the cases involving this company seem to reflect the gravest abuses and are very well reported and substantiated.

© The Author(s) 2018

C. Cole, R. Vermeltfoort, *U.S. Government Contractors and Human Trafficking*,
SpringerBriefs in Criminology, https://doi.org/10.1007/978-3-319-70827-0_1

from their home countries to Iraq through recruitment agents in the respective countries. These recruitment agents regularly use deceptive practices such as lying about employment terms and placement as well as charging exorbitant recruitment fees with return rates as high as 50% per year (Brown, 2007; ACLU & Yale Law School, 2012). In some cases, TCNs are not even aware that they are destined for Iraq until they are already on their way to transit hubs such as Dubai or Kuwait City (ACLU & Yale Law School, 2012). Upon arrival TCNs are frequently being subjected to a wide range of labor abuses likened by many authors to forced labor, modern slavery, and indentured servitude (see Brown, 2007; Stillman, 2011a; Goldberg, 2011). Reports include TCNs receiving a mere fraction of the salary that was promised to them, the withholding of passports, as well as being exposed to extremely poor living and working conditions and being forced to work up to 12 h a day for 7 days a week (Brown, 2007; Stillman, 2011a). It is estimated that some 250,000 TCNs have become victims of USG contractors up until today (Isenberg & Schwellenbach, 2011).

The allegations against KBR and their subcontractors are well substantiated and have been repeatedly addressed by the USG, under pressure by the multitude of reported incidents of trafficking and forced labor. However, to this date, there has not been a single case of a PMC being successfully prosecuted or fined for their involvement in human trafficking or labor abuses (ACLU & Yale Law School, 2012). KBR has continuously denied responsibility for these practices stating that they themselves and their subcontractors adhere to the law and USG Codes of Conduct (Brown, 2007). On the side of the USG, one could observe that more and more efforts are being made to stop the practices of human trafficking and forced labor and to protect TCNs. However, the US's "zero-tolerance policy" against human trafficking and the potential legal tools to prosecute or sanction government contractors have proven considerably weak and have created a culture of impunity when it comes to crimes of human trafficking and forced labor perpetrated by KBR and their subcontractors (ACLU & Yale Law School, 2012).

This thesis is aiming at revealing the dynamics and explanatory factors behind the crimes of human trafficking and forced labor perpetrated by KBR and their subcontractors. In order for the USG and the international community as a whole to properly legislate and react to this phenomenon, it is crucial to firstly understand the extent of these crimes and the legal framework surrounding them as well as the specific reasons for their commission. Identifying and analyzing these factors could significantly advance future efforts to combat TCN trafficking and forced labor, directing new regulations, policies, and legislative changes at crucial determinants enabling contractors to engage in these crimes.

Therefore, this thesis is dedicated at answering the following three research questions:

To what extent is the USG contractor KBR and their subcontractors involved in human trafficking and forced labor of TCNs in Iraq?

How are these contractors still able to engage in these crimes with impunity?
How can the involvement in human trafficking and forced labor by these contractors be explained criminologically?

1.1 Structure

This thesis is structured as follows: firstly, Chap. 2 provides background information on the development of the private military industry during the past decades. The history, different business sectors, and implications of the increased use of PMCs will be discussed followed by a depiction of PMCs in US-occupied Iraq particularly focusing on the role of KBR.

Subsequently, Chap. 3 aims at answering the first research question revealing the extent to which KBR and their subcontractors are involved in human trafficking and forced labor in Iraq. Herein, definitions of the crimes of human trafficking and forced labor will be provided, and it will be discussed whether these crimes could constitute international crimes. The following paragraphs will elaborate in depth on the situation of TCNs in Iraq depicting the recruitment process, TCNs' journey to Iraq, as well as their living and working conditions on-site. The role KBR and their subcontractors play in this process will be vividly illustrated by three well-documented cases of TCN trafficking and forced labor. Finally, the legal framework surrounding human trafficking and forced labor by USG contractors will be elucidated.

Answering the second research question of this thesis, Chap. 4 will outline the legal framework surrounding the crimes of human trafficking and forced labor by USG contractors and will show how the existing laws and regulations enable PMCs to continuously engage in these crimes with impunity.

Chapters 5 and 6 are dedicated to the third research question of this thesis where the reasons for PMC involvement in TCN trafficking and labor abuses will be explained on criminological grounds. For this purpose, state-corporate crime theory (Kramer, 1990a) as well as the integrative model of state-corporate crime (Kramer & Michalowski, 2006) will be presented in Chap. 5 and applied to the present case in the subsequent analysis in Chap. 6. Chapters 7 and 8 will draw conclusions and critically discuss the conducted research.

1.2 Method

The present thesis constitutes a case study research. Case studies aim at closely and intensively examining an issue for purposes of illumination and detailed understanding (Hays, 2004; Yin, 1994). Furthermore, case studies are utilized to "uncover new and unusual interactions, events, explanations, interpretations, and cause-and-effect connections" (Hays, 2004, pp. 218–219). As it is the aim of this thesis to reveal the extent to which specific actors, namely, KBR and their subcontractors, are involved in specific crimes, namely, TCN trafficking and forced labor, and to subsequently explain these crimes and ongoing impunity of the contractors, a case study research seems well suited for this endeavor. This method allows for a comprehensive overview and understanding of the specific issue at hand and to explore the specific dynamics of the case.

The research conducted for this study consists of a thorough and extensive literature review. Works by prominent criminological theorists, scholarly articles, as well as legal and policy documents were studied and analyzed. However, due to the relative scarcity of scholarly work on the specific topic at hand, many journalistic pieces and NGO reports were used and have proven crucial in order to get a proper overview of the issue. Therefore, some methodological limitations of the conducted research need to be acknowledged at this point.

Firstly, the reliability of journalistic articles and NGO reports could be questioned. Care needs to be taken when evaluating journalistic sources as the facts presented in these pieces can sometimes be poorly substantiated or exaggerated in order to provoke public attention or outrage. Furthermore, NGO reports could be influenced in a certain direction due to a political affiliation of the organization. This methodological consideration was kept in mind throughout the writing process of this thesis. In order to prevent the reliance on incorrect facts or biased information, the method of triangulation was used, analyzing and comparing various different sources on reported facts and incidents to thoroughly substantiate given information.

Secondly, it is crucial to note that despite extensive reporting and investigation by journalists, scholars, and NGOs, one cannot be certain that the openly available sources depict the total picture and whole truth about TCN trafficking and forced labor in Iraq. Therefore, conducting additional empirical research in the form of interviews with victims, experts, or potential perpetrators to complement the findings of the literature review would have undoubtedly been insightful and interesting. However, due to the sensitive and potentially perilous nature of the issue at hand, this endeavor has not been undertaken at this point.

1.3 Definitional Clarifications

At this point, it is crucial to provide some definitions of terms and key concepts reoccurring throughout this thesis. Firstly, it is important to note that hardly any author uses the term *PMC* the same way. Isenberg (2009) observes that there exists no officially recognized definition of the term and likens the controversy and confusion in this regard to a “definitional morass” (p. 14). As we will see below, there are a variety of different kinds of firms providing different kinds of military-related services to their clients ranging from actual combat to logistics services. It is therefore criticized that the term PMC is oftentimes used to include all private firms offering these services irrespective of their specific nature. It is therefore being argued that one should differentiate between PMCs, i.e., logistical and military consulting firms, and *PSCs* (short for "private security firms"), i.e., combat- and security-related companies (Isenberg, 2009).

For the purpose of this thesis, whenever the text not specifically refers to KBR or their subcontractors but rather to military-related service providers in general, the term PMCs will be used. The terms *USG contractors* or *private contractors* are used synonymously. The term *prime contractor* refers to a PMC that is in a direct contractual relationship with the USG, like KBR in Iraq. *Subcontractors* are companies that in turn are hired by prime contractors to carry out some of their contractual duties.

Chapter 2
The Private Military Industry

In order to answer the research questions of this thesis and thus explain to what extent, how, and why KBR and their subcontractors operating under USG contracts in Iraq continue to be involved in human trafficking and forced labor with impunity, it is crucial to highlight the rise and the dynamics of the private military industry in general, as well as the special and unprecedented role PMCs played in US-occupied Iraq. Therefore, this chapter will firstly elaborate on major factors contributing to the development and rise of the private military industry during the last decades. Secondly, the different business sectors of the industry will be briefly described, followed by a depiction of the implications and challenges resulting from the increased use of PMCs in military operations. Lastly, this section will elucidate the role of PMCs in US-occupied Iraq.

2.1 Toward the Privatization of Military Tasks

It is not a recent phenomenon that civilians accompany armed forces into war. Already during the American Civil War, World War II, and the US war in Vietnam, civilians played a significant role accompanying the troops and supporting military operations (Brown, 2007). However, in recent years, the number of civilian employees has risen to an unprecedented level, at some points even outnumbering the uniformed personnel in US war zones such as Iraq and Afghanistan (Brown, 2007; Li, 2015).

The significant expansion of the private military industry began in the early 1990s after the end of the Cold War and can be explained by three underlying major developments gradually intertwining the public and private sectors in respect to military operations (Singer, 2001, 2004). Firstly, Singer (2001) contends that the dynamics after the end of the Cold War era led to a vacuum in the market of security characterized by growing global instability and the emergence of new or lingering conflicts paired with a radical downsizing of professional state armed forced. After

© The Author(s) 2018
C. Cole, R. Vermeltfoort, *U.S. Government Contractors and Human Trafficking*, SpringerBriefs in Criminology, https://doi.org/10.1007/978-3-319-70827-0_2

the Cold War, the world's armies shrank by over six million individuals with the United States alone reducing its active forces from 2.2 million in 1989 to 1.38 million in 2000 (Singer, 2001; Ortiz, 2004). This radical downsizing left millions of highly qualified former soldiers seeking for employment that many of them found in the ranks of a variety of newly established PMCs (Ortiz, 2004). Simultaneously, the security priorities of states, especially those of the superpowers, significantly shifted, leading to an increased unwillingness to intervene with their own state armed forces in areas of political instability as "conflicts in many developing regions no longer pose serious threats to the national interests of these powers" (Singer, 2001, p. 10). Sending state troops to intervene against diffuse enemies abroad and thus risking high numbers of troop casualties became less and less desirable, particularly after events such as the live broadcasted killing of US soldiers in Somalia, which outraged the public and significantly decreased popular support for such endeavors. These dynamics left a void to fill for the newly emerged, highly qualified PMCs readily offering their professional military services to clients in need.

Secondly, Singer (2001) identifies the changing nature of warfare as a major contributing factor for the rise of PMCs and their predicted importance for future military operations. In recent years, military operations, especially those led by the great powers, have become strongly technology based, utilizing complex and sophisticated combat systems that can only be provided and operated by highly specialized private companies. Evidently, this makes the military more and more reliant on actors from the private sector as only trained specialists can provide the technological expertise required (Singer, 2001, 2004). Experts contend that the US Army will not be able to keep up its modern systems during warfare without employing private contractors even in the close combat area (Singer, 2001).

Lastly, the ideological push for governmental privatization and outsourcing is considered crucial for the significant expansion of the private military industry. Based on the underlying assumption that the private sector could handle tasks more quickly and efficiently, there has emerged a trend in the past few decades to privatize any function that can be provided from outside the government (Singer, 2001). After some major success in privatizing institutions that were initially exclusively handled by the state like schools, prisons, and the policing sector, Singer (2001, 2004) contends that it was only a matter of time that military services would become subject to privatization as well, creating a new space and manifold employment opportunities for PMCs.

2.2 Business Branches in the Private Military Industry

The private military industry is more diverse than one would initially assume with different kinds of PMCs offering different kinds of military-related services. Singer (2001) divides the industry into three basic business sectors: (1) military provider firms, (2) military consulting firms, and (3) military support firms. Military provider firms are companies offering direct military or security assistance to clients, including the engagement in actual frontline combat, tactical assistance, and direct command (Singer, 2001). These firms are often hired by clients with weak armed forces facing an immediate threat. Thus, the firms' employees frequently fight among a client's force to strengthen their efforts in combat and to provide expertise and leadership. A classic example of a military provider firm carrying out military missions throughout Africa is the South African company "Executive Outcomes."

The second type of companies, military consulting firms, consists mostly of retired senior military officials and specialists of different professions providing strategic advice and training services. Clients of these companies are usually in the process of restructuring their forces or aiming at acquiring special skills (Singer, 2001). The main difference between military provider firms and military consulting firms is the so-called "trigger finger" factor, as the latter do not directly participate in combat activities but rather act in the background of military operations educating and advising troops over a longer period of time. Military consulting firms also offer services and expertise that the military does not regularly possess, such as operating highly specialized surveillance technologies or drones (Singer, 2001). As stated by Isenberg (2009), the line between military provider firms and military consulting firms is gradually blurring, with some military consulting firms such as the US company "Blackwater" expanding into offering personal security and bodyguard services in Iraq.

Thirdly, military support firms are companies that do not participate in combat or the training of military personnel but provide functional support for deployed troops such as logistics, transport, intelligence, and maintenance services. Outsourcing these tasks to private companies allows military personnel to fully concentrate on combat activities and helps administrations to reduce the official number of deployed government troops to a war zone, a highly political decision directly linked to public support for a military mission (Singer, 2001, 2004). Clients of military support firms are usually engaged in long-term interventions or occupation scenarios such as the US occupation of Iraq and subsequent military presence in the country (Singer, 2001). As outlined throughout this thesis, the company KBR operating in Iraq is a vivid example of a military support firm.

2.3 Implications of the Increased Privatization of Military Tasks

The quick rise of the private military industry resulting in the deployment of thousands of private contractors to war zones worldwide did not come without consequences and serious implications for the international security domain. Especially during the Iraq war era, when an unprecedented number of private contractors were hired by the USG, major dilemmas surrounding the use of PMCs gradually surfaced (Singer, 2004, 2011).

The first serious concern voiced by Singer (2004) is the likely occurring conflict of interest between private contractors and their clients. The primary motivation for PMCs to enter into contractual relations with a client is to make maximum profit, whereas clients will pursue the goal of winning a war and establishing or maintaining peace in a conflict-ridden area. This incentive to turn profit has already led to a series of contractual overcharging and war-profiteering allegations against PMCs. Furthermore, the conflict of interest between PMCs and their clients can easily lead to tensions between contractor employees and the local population, obscuring a client's peace-building or peacekeeping efforts. Illustrating this issue, it has been widely reported that in US-occupied Iraq, employees of the private contractor Blackwater used to treat the local population highly disrespectful and degrading, declaring that it was their mission to protect their clients, not to "...win Iraqi hearts and minds along the way" (Singer, 2007, p. 6). In contrast, US soldiers were apparently making more positive efforts with the Iraqi civilian population (Singer, 2007).

Another important issue of concern regarding the private military industry is that the market is effectively unregulated with insufficient screening processes and controls over whom PMCs recruit and hire. As mentioned above, the majority of PMC employees have a highly professional and prestigious military background. However, as revealed in the 2003 Abu Ghraib prison abuse scandal, the lack of control and adequate screening can lead to firms hiring individuals with questionable backgrounds that never received any formal military training (Singer, 2004).

Furthermore, the increased use of private contractors in war zones has led to a lack of transparency regarding military operations abroad. Singer (2004) substantiates this assumption by illustrating that the incentive for the USG to resort to PMCs to such a large extent during the Iraq occupation was a highly political decision. By covertly hiring PMCs instead of sending more US soldiers to Iraq, further public division and dissent concerning the war could be avoided as the broad public was left uninformed about this development. Singer (2007) contends that "the American public remains largely unaware of the industry. While private forces make up over 50% of the overall operation in Iraq, they have been mentioned in only a quarter of one percent of all American media stories" (p. 5). The fact that private contractors are regularly left out of official statistics on military deaths undercuts transparency even further, with the public left with no clue about the actual death toll of the war (Singer, 2004). As a responsible, accountable, and transparent government is considered one of the fundamental principles of a functioning democracy, this development raises serious concerns.

Finally, one of the most alarming and widely discussed problems concerning the private military industry is the lack of legal accountability and effective law enforcement when it comes to crimes committed by PMC employees. As this issue will be discussed in depth in subsequent parts of this thesis, it suffices to state at this point that PMCs fall into a legal gray area with a high level of uncertainty concerning applicable laws and jurisdictional matters (Brown, 2007; Singer, 2004).

2.4 The Role of PMCs in Iraq

As previously elucidated, the rise of the private military industry already began after the Cold War era. However, in the early 2000s with the US-led intervention in Iraq, the largest US military commitment since World War II, the reliance on private contractors assumed an unprecedented level (Singer, 2004; Isenberg, 2009).

2.4.1 Facts and Figures

Published estimates of the number of contractor personnel in Iraq differ significantly depending on the source, and the reliability of the data has been questioned repeatedly (Moyer, 2011; Schwartz & Swain, 2011). An official and thoroughly researched report issued in 2011 by the US Congressional Research Service (CRS) stated that as of March 2011, approximately 64,000 Department of Defense (DoD) contractor employees were present in Iraq outnumbering the 46,000 uniformed personnel (Schwartz & Swain, 2011). This means that 58% of the total US workforce present in Iraq in 2011 consisted of private contractors.

The number of both contractors and troops constantly declined leading up to the withdrawal of US troops in 2011 (Fig. 2.1). Four years earlier in 2007, the number of contractor personnel was at its height with estimates ranging between 160,000 and 180,000 individuals working in the country (Singer, 2007; Moyer, 2011; Schwartz &

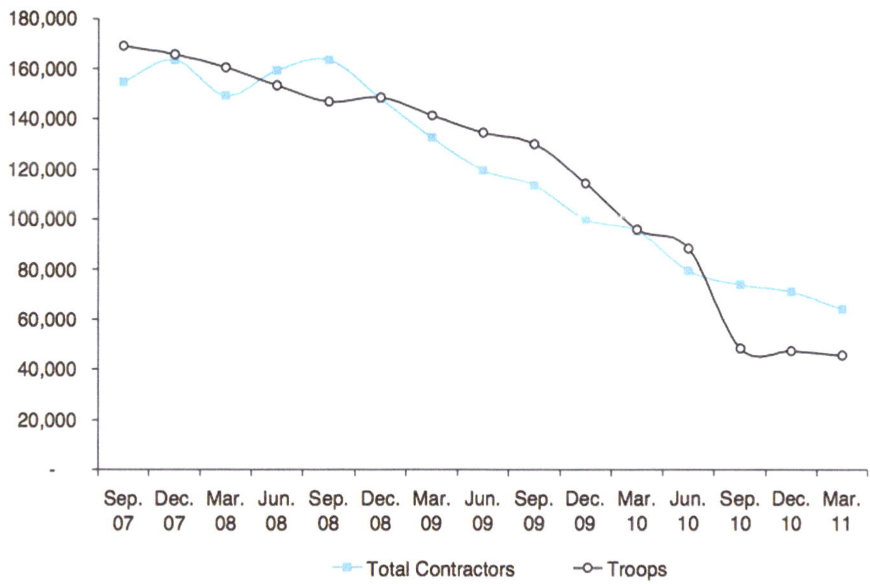

Fig. 2.1 Number of contractor personnel in Iraq vs. troop levels (Schwartz & Swain, 2011, p. 9)

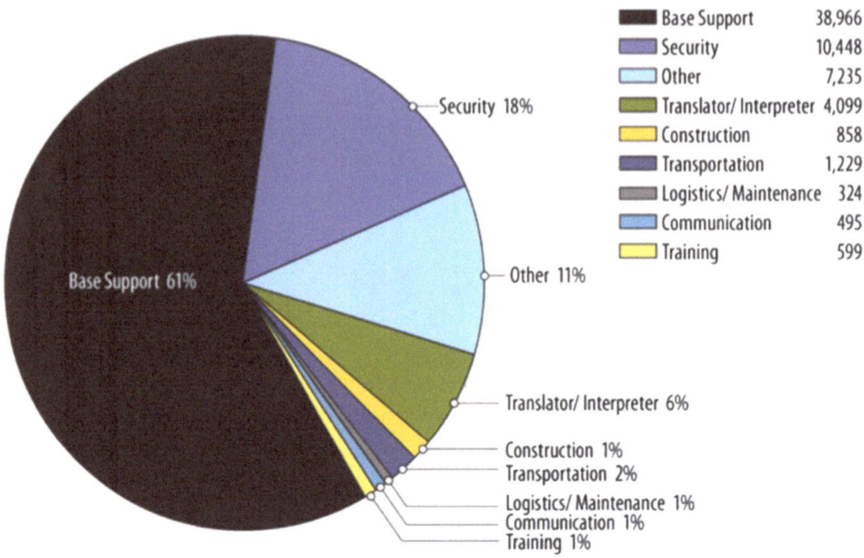

Fig. 2.2 Contractor personnel in Iraq by type of service provided (Schwartz & Swain 2011, p. 16)

Swain, 2011). In the years following the withdrawal of US troops in December 2011, several thousands of contractor employees remained in the country carrying out "translator/interpreter, transportation, logistics or maintenance functions" (Peters, Schwartz, & Kapp, 2015, p. 6; Li, 2015).

Not only the large number of personnel but also the wide scope of tasks carried out by private contractors was a remarkable development during the US occupation of Iraq (Singer, 2004). In addition to field training, combat duties, and the provision of security services, a large number of contractors were in charge of translation services, logistics, construction or maintenance duties, and most prominently military base support (Singer, 2004; Schwartz & Swain, 2011). As of March 2011, 61% of contractor personnel worked in base support, only 18% in security services, with the remaining 21% being distributed among the remaining tasks (Fig. 2.2).

2.4.2 *KBR in Iraq*

KBR is a Houston-based global technology, engineering, procurement, and construction company founded in 1998. Until 2006, the company has been a subsidiary of the oil company Halliburton run by Dick Cheney who was appointed US Vice President (VP) under the Bush administration in 2001. Halliburton has for a long time been a controversially debated company with repeated allegations of corporate malfeasance such as accounting fraud, bribery, corruption, and illegal overcharging for contractual services. The amount of money the company has been accused of overcharging the USG is estimated at $1.8 billion (Singer, 2004; Rothe, 2006). Furthermore, the company has been repeatedly investigated due to accusations of utilizing loopholes to circumvent US trade law or international sanctions in order to profit from business with the Saddam Hussein regime and Iran (Rothe, 2006).

In addition to Halliburton's dubious business history, Dick Cheney's ongoing ties to the company after he became VP have been sharply criticized. Former CEO Cheney's appointment to one of the highest government functions can be regarded as a perfect example of the "revolving door effect," a term introduced by Mills (1956) to describe the phenomenon of the increased entanglement of corporate and state interests when corporate actors eventually obtain government positions (Rothe, 2006). Cheney has repeatedly stated that he completely severed his ties with Halliburton upon his appointment as VP, but investigations revealed that he still owned large amounts of company shares (Rothe, 2006).

Before the 2003 military mission to Iraq began, Halliburton-subsidiary KBR was granted an open-ended contract for troop supply, logistics, and base construction services wherever US troops would go for the next 10 years. During the next decade, KBR would earn an estimated $39.5 billion for their services in Iraq and would be the company that by far made most profits during the Iraq war (Young, 2013). Under the DoD's Logistics Civil Augmentation Program III (LOGCAP III) contracts, KBR was responsible for managing the supply of logistical needs for the mission, including the provision of transport, food, and cleaning services, as well as the recruitment and hiring of military base support workers. KBR soon began outsourcing considerable parts of its contracts, including the recruitment of workers for the military bases, to subcontractors in Middle Eastern nations (Li, 2015; Singer, 2007).

2.4.3 Lessons Learned

In retrospect and with all the discussed issues and scandals in mind that occurred throughout the last decade, the excessive commitment of private contractors in Iraq has been widely and publicly criticized, even by sources within the USG. A 2013 CRS report thoroughly analyzed the use of PMCs in past military operations, closely examining past commitments and suggesting necessary and long overdue changes regarding the proper use, oversight, and control of hired PMCs in future operations (Schwartz & Church, 2013). The report clearly states that the DoD admits of having been insufficiently prepared to rely on PMCs on such a large scale as in Iraq and that "the use of contractors was done on an ad-hoc basis, without significant consideration of implications for foreign policy and without putting in place the necessary oversight" (Schwartz & Church, 2013, p. 5). It is further recognized that this lack of preparation and control resulted in numerous cases of poor performance, fraudulent behavior, billions of dollars of waste, and failure to achieve mission goals (Schwartz & Church, 2013).

On the side of the USG, it can definitely be considered a step in the right direction to identify and acknowledge what has gone wrong in Iraq. However, as will become evident throughout this thesis, when it comes to dealing with abuses and crimes committed by private contractors in Iraq, not least because of insufficient control and oversight, the USG has yet to implement appropriate and effective regulations and adequate legal instruments.

Chapter 3
Human Trafficking and Forced Labor of TCNs in Iraq

In order to elucidate the extent to which KBR and its subcontractors are involved in human trafficking and forced labor in Iraq, the subsequent chapter of this thesis will elaborate in depth on the situation of TCNs and on documented cases of TCN trafficking and forced labor by several KBR subcontractors.

Firstly, internationally recognized definitions of the crimes of human trafficking and forced labor will be given, and the potential accommodation of these crimes under the concept of international crimes will be elucidated. Subsequently, an in-depth description of the situation of TCNs in Iraq, including typical backgrounds and profiles of TCNs, the recruiting process, as well as usual living and working conditions will be given followed by a presentation of some of the most well-reported cases of TCN trafficking and forced labor in Iraq.

3.1 The Crimes of Human Trafficking and Forced Labor

3.1.1 Definitions

In order to properly determine whether the subsequently discussed practices and cases in fact constitute crimes of human trafficking and forced labor, it is firstly crucial to legally define these crimes. Internationally recognized definitions of human trafficking and forced labor by the United Nations Organization (UNO) and the International Labor Organization (ILO) as well as definitions of the crimes under US law will be provided.

© The Author(s) 2018

C. Cole, R. Vermeltfoort, *U.S. Government Contractors and Human Trafficking*, SpringerBriefs in Criminology, https://doi.org/10.1007/978-3-319-70827-0_3

3.1.1.1 Human Trafficking

The United Nations Protocol to Prevent, Suppress and Punish Trafficking in Persons (2000), also known as the Palermo Protocol, defines human trafficking as:

> … the recruitment, transportation, transfer, harboring or receipt of persons, by means of the threat or use of force or other forms of coercion, of abduction, of fraud, of deception, of the abuse of power or of a position of vulnerability or of the giving or receiving of payments or benefits to achieve the consent of a person having control over another person, for the purpose of exploitation. Exploitation shall include, at a minimum, the exploitation of the prostitution of others or other forms of sexual exploitation, forced labor or services, slavery or practices similar to slavery, servitude or the removal of organs. (Art. 3 (a))

US legislation defines human trafficking similarly as:

> (a) sex trafficking in which a commercial sex act is induced by force, fraud, or coercion, or in which the person induced to perform such act has not attained 18 years of age; or (b) the recruitment, harboring, transportation, provision, or obtaining of a person for labor or services, through the use of force, fraud, or coercion[1] for the purpose of subjection to involuntary servitude, peonage, debt bondage, or slavery.
>
> (22 U.S. Code § 7102 (9) (A,B))

The broad and comprehensive definition provided by the Palermo Protocol is the internationally recognized definition of human trafficking. The definition covers the three constituent elements of human trafficking: (1) the act (recruitment, transportation, transfer, harboring, and the receipt of persons), (2) the means (threat or use of force, coercion, abduction, fraud, deception, abuse of power and vulnerability, giving payments and benefits), and (3) the purpose (exploitation in the form of prostitution, sexual exploitation, forced labor, slavery, removal of organs, and other forms of exploitation) (UNODC, 2016). The purpose of this definition was to provide consistency and consensus among member states as to what constitutes the crime of human trafficking and to provide a basis for member states' incorporation of the defined conduct into domestic criminal legislation. However, member states are not urged to adopt the exact wording of the UNO definition but rather to adapt it in accordance with the respective domestic legal system.

The US legal definition of human trafficking introduced by the Trafficking Victims Protection Act (TVPA) in 2000 explicitly distinguishes between sex trafficking and labor trafficking equally criminalizing both forms. For the most part, the US definition uses similar language as the Palermo Protocol. However, the TVPA does not criminalize human trafficking for the purpose of organ removal—a fact that is sharply criticized by legal scholars (see Pugliese, 2007).

[1] The term "coercion" explicitly includes forms of nonviolent coercion, such as creating an environment of fear and intimidation preventing workers from leaving exploitative working situations (ACLU & Yale Law School, 2012). See 22 US Code §7102 (3).

3.1.1.2 Forced Labor

The Forced Labor Convention adopted by the International Labor Organization (ILO) in 1930 defines forced labor as:

> ...all work or service which is exacted from any person under the menace of any penalty and for which the said person has not offered himself voluntarily. (Art. 2 (1))

Furthermore, in 2012, the ILO published a comprehensive guidebook identifying 11 indicators of forced labor covering the main possible elements of a forced labor situation to further specify the convention's definition: (1) abuse of vulnerability, (2) deception, (3) restriction of movement, (4) isolation, (5) physical and sexual violence, (6) intimidation or threats, (7) retention of identity papers, (8) withholding of wages, (9) debt bondage, (10) abusive work and living conditions, and (11) excessive overtime (ILO, 2012).

On this basis, in 2014, the ILO characterized forced labor situations as:

> ... situations in which persons are coerced to work through the use of violence or intimidation, or by more subtle means such as accumulated debt, retention of identity papers or threats of denunciation to immigration authorities. (ILO, 2014, para. 1)

Up until today, the 1930 Forced Labor Convention has not been ratified by the United States due to disagreements on a particular provision concerning the subcontracting of prison labor (USCIB, 2007). Of the eight ILO core conventions, the United States has only ratified two stating that ratification and thus an adoption of the conventions' provisions into domestic law would "directly conflict with [longstanding principles of] U.S. law and practice and would require significant and widespread changes to U.S. state and federal law if they were ratified)" (USCIB, 2007, p. 3). However, the United States has ratified the 1957 Abolition of Forced Labor Convention committing to the cause of combatting forced labor, and in 2000, the TVPA introduced new legislation to criminalize forced labor under US domestic law. Although not as comprehensive as the definition and indicators provided by the ILO, the US law now covers some of the most serious forced labor situations.

The US law considers a person guilty of charges of forced labor who:

> ... knowingly provides or obtains the labor or services of a person by any one of, or by any combination of, the following means:
>
> (1) by means of force, threats of force, physical restraint, or threats of physical restraint to that person or another person;
> (2) by means of serious harm or threats of serious harm to that person or another person;
> (3) by means of the abuse or threatened abuse of law or legal process; or
> (4) by means of any scheme, plan, or pattern intended to cause the person to believe that, if that person did not perform such labor or services, that person or another person would suffer serious harm or physical restraint.
>
> (18 U.S. Code §1589 (a) (1-4))

3.1.2 *Human Trafficking and Forced Labor as International Crimes*

As concerns international crimes), human trafficking and forced labor could fall under Art. 7 (1) (c) of the Rome Statute of the International Criminal Court (ICC), which lists "enslavement" as a crime against humanity. Article 7 (2) (c) defines "enslavement" as follows:

> 'Enslavement' means the exercise of any or all of the powers attaching to the right of ownership over a person and includes the exercise of such power in the course of trafficking in persons, in particular women and children.

This definition is further elaborated in Article 7 (1) (c) of the ICC's Elements of Crimes stating that enslavement entails that:

> The perpetrator exercised any or all of the powers attaching to the right of ownership over one or more persons, such as by purchasing, selling, lending or bartering such a person or persons, or by imposing on them a similar deprivation of liberty.

The term "similar deprivation of liberty" is further elaborated in a footnote stating that in some circumstances, it can include forced labor and trafficking in persons. Accordingly, the crimes of human trafficking and forced labor could be seen as a crime against humanity provided that the central underlying assumption of crimes against humanity, a widespread and systematic attack against a civilian population, can be proven.

However, when considering the definition of the crime of enslavement provided above, it becomes clear that there exist considerable difficulties with regard to the ICC's prosecution of human trafficking and forced labor under this provision. Neither the ICC Statute nor the ICC's Elements of Crimes provide a clear definition of human trafficking and forced labor. This is highly problematic and constitutes the biggest impediment concerning the prosecution of trafficking cases by the ICC (Aston & Paranjape, 2012). As we could see in Sect. 3.1.1.1, the definition of human trafficking provided by the 2000 Palermo Protocol is very precise, and the ICC has been urged by several authors to adopt this definition (Aston & Paranjape, 2012; Schiff, 2008). The lack of effective definitional clarification is further illustrated by the fact that Article 7 (1) (c) of the ICC's Elements of Crimes states that "in some circumstances" forced labor and human trafficking could fall under the term "similar deprivation of liberty." These circumstances, however, are not further defined.

Concluding the abovementioned facts, one can observe that although human trafficking and forced labor could possibly fall under Article 7 (1) (c) of the ICC Statute, actual prosecution of these crimes would prove highly difficult due to a lack of clear legal definitions in the ICC Statute and Elements of Crimes.

3.2 The Situation of TCNs in Iraq

As elaborated above, the number of private contractors in Iraq was unprecedented in military history with some 64,000 employees being present in the country as of March 2011. Remarkably, of these 64,000 individuals, 57% (37,000) were TCNs. Only 18,000 US citizens and 9,000 Iraqi nationals were among the contractor employees (Schwartz & Swain, 2011).

The following paragraph will discuss the situation of this considerable workforce in Iraq revealing a long-standing pattern of TCN trafficking and labor abuses committed by USG contractor KBR and their subcontractors.

3.2.1 Who Are TCNs?

TCNs are frequently referred to as "the army behind the army" as they constitute the "largest and most diverse civilian workforce ever assembled in support of U.S. military operations abroad" (ACLU & Yale Law School, 2012, p. 19). TCNs usually come from low-income countries such as Sri Lanka, Nepal, India, the Philippines, Uganda, and Fiji[2] and are hired to perform low-wage jobs at military bases such as construction, cleaning, and food services (ACLU & Yale Law School, 2012; Li, 2015). Often coming from poor, rural areas with a lack of employment opportunities and extremely low wages, an offer to work abroad seems to constitute the chance of a lifetime for TCNs struggling to provide for their families (ACLU & Yale Law School, 2012). As these individuals are mostly uneducated and inexperienced in working abroad and suffer from considerable financial insecurity, they are highly vulnerable to abuse and exploitation by fraudulent recruitment agents (ACLU & Yale Law School, 2012; Li, 2015).

3.2.2 The Recruitment of TCNs

As illustrated in Sect. 2.4.2. of this thesis, in 2003, KBR was awarded the highly lucrative LOGCAP III contracts by the DoD to manage the supply of logistical needs for the entire military mission in Iraq. The company soon began to manage the numerous and manifold tasks of the contract by outsourcing a considerable part of its duties, including the recruitment of workers for the military bases, to more than 200 local subcontractors in Middle Eastern nations (Brown, 2007). These local

[2] There is no publicly available data concerning demographic details of TCNs. However, the listed countries are most frequently reported as TCN home countries.

subcontractors commonly hire corrupt recruitment agents in TCN home countries who use fraudulent schemes to recruit large numbers of TCNs. Thus, the recruitment process in TCN home countries is usually characterized by exorbitant recruitment fees, deceptive promises concerning the compensation of the future job, and misrepresentations of the nature and conditions of the work (ACLU & Yale Law School, 2012).

It is reported that recruitment agents regularly charge applicants a recruitment fee between $1000 and 5000, a considerable sum of money for individuals in low-income countries like India, where on average families earn as little as $1 per day (ACLU & Yale Law School, 2012). Oftentimes, additional fees are charged by the agents for special training classes allegedly required for the prospective job that in the end turns out to be useless.

One of the gravest problems associated with these exorbitant recruitment fees is the fact that the vast majority of TCNs is forced to borrow the required money from loan sharks or illicit lenders (Brown, 2007; ACLU & Yale Law School, 2012). These lenders regularly demand interest rates of 30–50% per year and use intimidation tactics and violence in order to retrieve their money. As TCNs most likely earn less in their prospective jobs than they were led to believe by recruitment agents, many find themselves unable to repay the loan sharks on time resulting in numerous reported incidents of severe physical and psychological violence directed against the family of TCNs at home (ACLU & Yale Law School, 2012). Having been promised wages ten times higher than they actually make in Iraq, TCNs frequently have to work up to 2 years just to repay their loans at home without being able to keep any money for themselves. This situation was likened to a relationship of indentured servitude and slave labor by several authors (see Brown, 2007; ACLU & Yale Law School, 2012; Kavinnamannil & McCahon, 2011).

Furthermore, it has frequently been reported by TCNs that during the recruitment process, they were left unaware of the fact that they are destined for Iraq to work on a US military base. Agents apparently tend to misrepresent the nature and location of TCNs' prospective jobs promising safe, lucrative, and attractive work in hotels in Kuwait, United Arab Emirates, Jordan, or Saudi Arabia (Stillman 2011a; ACLU & Yale Law School, 2012). ACLU & Yale Law School, (2012) recalls an Indian individual stating that an estimated 90% of the fellow workers in his camp were left unaware of the fact that the location of their job was Iraq.

The hierarchy in the recruitment of TCNs for military bases in Iraq is depicted in Fig. 3.1. This complex chain of relationships and the multitude of actors involved in the recruitment process pose severe challenges to control, oversight, and attributing criminal liability and thus to holding contractors accountable for human trafficking and forced labor.

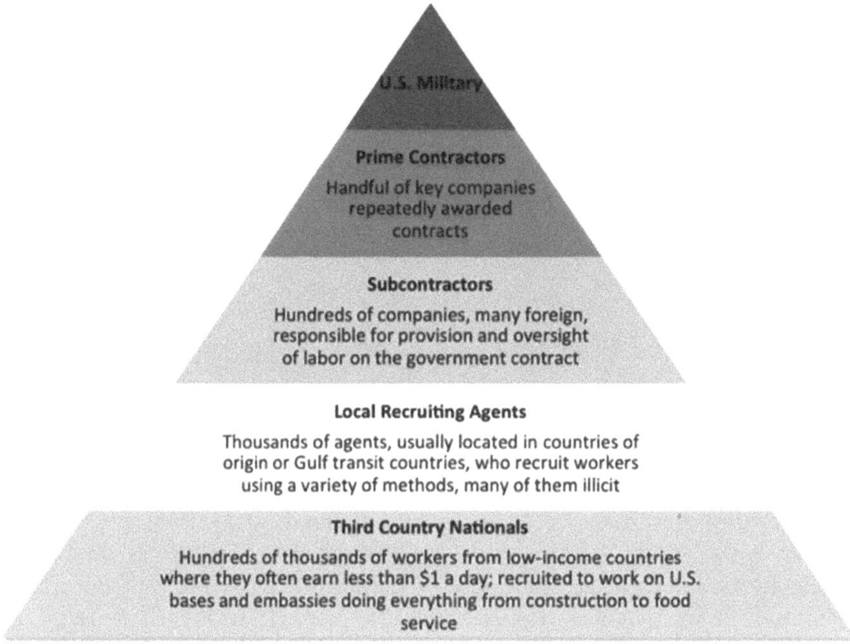

Fig. 3.1 Recruitment hierarchy (ACLU & Yale Law School, 2012, p. 68)

3.2.3 TCNs' Journey to Iraq

After the recruiting process, TCNs embark on their journey to Iraq via transit hubs such as Dubai or Kuwait City where local subcontractors are located. It is mostly during this transit period that the abusive treatment begins, and TCNs become aware of their predicament (ACLU & Yale Law School, 2012).

During transit, many TCNs who were previously left in the dark about their final destination become aware that they are bound for Iraq and consequently request that the subcontractors return them back home. Several reports state that in such cases, TCNs were coerced into going to Iraq with subcontractors confiscating their passports and threatening to abandon them at the transit hub with no means to survive (Stillman, 2011a; ACLU & Yale Law School, 2012). Other TCNs finding out that they are destined for Iraq quietly agree and go along out of fear of being unable to repay the previously lent money if the prospective job falls through (Simpson, 2005; Stillman, 2011a).

At transit hubs, TCNs are furthermore frequently held against their will in filthy and overcrowded accommodations for several months without pay before they reach Iraq (Al Jazeera, 2014). Upon arrival in Iraq, similar conditions await many TCNs, whose passports are being seized and who have to wait for months before obtaining employment and eventually being paid. This tactic was termed "warehousing workers" and allows contractors "to fill vacancies without needing to restart the entire recruitment process" (ACLU & Yale Law School, 2012, p. 24). These practices delay the repayment of workers' debts for months on end and even force many deeply indebted and vulnerable TCNs to return home without having earned any money.

3.2.4 Living and Working Conditions

Once TCNs start their jobs at Iraqi military bases, abuses continue, particularly in the form of unbearable living and working conditions. TCNs usually live in so-called man camps, mostly run by KBR subcontractors, near the military bases where they work (Stillman, 2011a; ACLU & Yale Law School, 2012). These camps, often housing thousands of workers, have repeatedly been described as unsanitary, extremely overcrowded, and lacking air conditioning as well as sufficient bathrooms and shower facilities (Rohde, 2004; Stillman, 2011a; ACLU & Yale Law School, 2012). Furthermore, TCN statements show that many workers lack access to proper food, being forced to eat spoiled meals or leftovers from the soldiers. One reported incident even stated that TCNs were ordered "to eat leftover food off of dirt floors, as well as out of a trough similar to pig farms" (ACLU & Yale Law School, 2012, p. 29).

Moreover, in the man camps, TCNs are significantly restricted in their freedom of movement, with managers forbidding them to leave the camps and cutting off any communication with the outside world. These prisonlike conditions go even further as TCNs often have limited access to communication facilities and extremely limited phone time per month. Reportedly, even American contractor employees and soldiers are not allowed to enter the camps and interact with TCNs (ACLU & Yale Law School, 2012).

TCNs usual working conditions are equally striking. Various TCNs have reported regular working hours between 12 and 16 h, no overtime payment, and no time off for considerable periods of time (ACLU & Yale Law School, 2012). Physical and verbal abuse of TCNs by supervisors as well as racial discrimination appears to be a common practice at Iraqi military bases (Rohde, 2004; Stillman, 2011a; ACLU & Yale Law School, 2012). Regularly, workers have been intimidated not to complain about their living and working conditions to military personnel by KBR managers, and when an American KBR employee started speaking out about the grave situation of TCNs, he was harshly reprimanded by the company (Stillman, 2011b).

3.2.5 *Conclusion*

When considering all the abovementioned information, it becomes clear that USG contractor KBR, subcontractors, and recruitment agents in countries of origin systematically exploit the desperate economic situation and vulnerability of TCNs, making them subject to a series of abuses throughout their recruiting process and upon arrival in Iraq. Demanding exorbitant recruitment fees, making deceptive promises about the nature and location of the jobs and intimidating TCNs have become common practices among local recruitment agents hired by KBR subcontractors to lure cheap workers into Iraq. The subcontractors regularly withhold passports of TCNs leading to a complete dependence on their employers. In case TCNs complain about their poor payments or living and working conditions, they are oftentimes intimidated or threatened by their superiors.

With regard to the definitions of the crimes of human trafficking and forced labor provided above, one can safely contend that these practices fit the elements of both the UNO and ILO definitions and the US definitions of human trafficking and forced labor. One could further argue that, despite the lack of definitional clarity in the ICC Statute, the committed crimes constitute crimes against humanity as human trafficking, and forced labor could potentially fall under Article 7 (1) (c) of the ICC Statute. For this to be the case, a widespread and systematic attack against a civilian population would need to be proven.

One could validly argue that the practices in question constitute such a widespread and systematic attack, as the trafficking and forced labor of TCNs have been going on for a substantial period of time and have schematically victimized tens of thousands of individuals in various countries. However, whether a court of law would deem the involvement of USG contractors in human trafficking and forced labor, a crime against humanity is hard to predict, and answering this question would go beyond the scope of this thesis. In any case, it can safely be contended that the trafficking and forced labor of TCNs constitute cases of gross human rights violations.

3.3 Documented Cases of TCN Trafficking and Forced Labor

The subsequent paragraph will briefly elaborate on three well-documented cases of TCN trafficking and forced labor in Iraq involving KBR and several of the company's subcontractors. The three cases were chosen as they nicely illustrate the common practices of TCN trafficking and forced labor described in the previous paragraphs.

3.3.1 Daoud and Partners

In 2005, the first incident involving allegations of human trafficking and forced labor against KBR and one of their subcontractors surfaced: in early 2004, 13 Nepali workers who were trafficked or lured to Iraq under deceptive promises were kidnapped, and 12 of them subsequently executed by terrorists on their way from Jordan to Iraq (Simpson, 2005; ACLU & Yale Law School, 2012). Reportedly, the Nepali men were recruited by local recruitment agencies that were working for the KBR subcontractor Daoud & Partners (hereafter Daoud) based in Dubai. The majority of the men were not aware that they were destined for Iraq but were promised well-paying jobs in a luxury hotel in Amman, Jordan. Upon arrival in Jordan, the workers were put on an unprotected caravan of vehicles heading to Al Asad Airbase in Iraq. En route, the caravan was ambushed by militants of the Ansar Al-Sunna army, who subsequently recorded and aired a video message showing the 12 men's execution. The only survivor was not allowed to return home after the attack but was reportedly forced to stay in Iraq by KBR and Daoud (Simpson, 2005; ACLU & Yale Law School, 2012; Smallteacher, 2014). The attack was apparently carried out in the context of a broader plan by Al Qaeda and other militant groups who in 2004 started deliberately targeting TCNs in order to "disrupt American supply chains [...] and to punish Third World Muslims who collaborated with the infidels" (Stillman, 2011a, para. 25).

In 2008, a lawsuit was brought against KBR and Daoud on behalf of the victims' families and the Nepali individual who survived the ambush. The suit was brought forward under the Alien Tort Claims Act (ATCA) and the Trafficking Victims Protection Reauthorization Act (TVPRA) and was initially accepted for trial in the US District Court. However, shortly after the initially set trial date in April 2014, the court revised its decision stating that the ATCA is not applicable in this case and that the TVPRA cannot be applied retroactively to incidents that occurred before the law was amended to include extraterritorial claims in 2005[3] (Adhikari v. Daoud & Partners 2014; Smallteacher, 2014). The case against KBR and Daoud remains the first and only human trafficking- or forced labor-related lawsuit brought forward against government contractors up until today.

3.3.2 Najlaa International Catering Services

In 2008, further allegations of trafficking and labor abuses emerged against KBR and its Kuwaiti subcontractor Najlaa International Catering Services (hereafter Najlaa). According to various sources, Najlaa had hired more than 1000 men from Sri Lanka, India, Nepal, and Bangladesh and confined them in a windowless warehouse near the Baghdad airport with no money or place to work for up to 3 months.

[3] For further elaboration on the legal framework surrounding the case, see Sect. 3.4 of this thesis.

The men were forced to live under extremely poor living conditions with only 12 functioning toilets and scarce rations of food. Some men even had to camp outside the warehouse in provisional tents along the airport road (Ashton, 2008; Isenberg & Schwellenbach, 2011). Apparently, the men were hired for contracts that eventually fell through due to disagreements between KBR and Najlaa. After the workers staged protests complaining about their situation, Najlaa eventually repatriated them, sending them home with only a fraction of the money the workers had to borrow to pay the recruitment fees of up to $5000 upon departure (ACLU & Yale Law School, 2012). Initially expecting to make enough money to pay back their debts at home and provide for their families by sending back money, these workers were forced to return to a desperate economic situation. After the incident became public, Najlaa received a further multimillion-dollar contract to run a dining facility in Iraq (Stillman 2011a).

3.3.3 Kulak Construction Company

In June 2011, the magazine *The New Yorker* featured a story by reporter Sarah Stillman about several Fijian women who had been approached by local recruiters in their village in 2007, promising them well-paid jobs as beauticians in Dubai (Stillman, 2011a). Upon arrival in Dubai, the women were met by a representative of the Turkish KBR subcontractor Kulak Construction Company (hereafter Kulak) and soon realized that they were bound for Iraq. After considering an escape, the women decided that they had no other chance than accepting their fate due to the loans they had taken up at home. Once the women arrived in Iraq, they were taken to work at Camp Anaconda, a US military base known for being frequently targeted by mortar fire (Stillman, 2011a). There, Kulak representatives told the women that they are going to earn only $700 per month, less than a half of the $1500 that were previously promised to them.

Furthermore, the women were made to sign a contract in Iraq, specifying their work hours as 12 h a day and 7 days a week. Kulak attached a waiver to the contract for the women to sign stating that they came to Iraq out of their own free will, that no one in Fiji had approached them with a job offer, that they are happy with their jobs, and that they would stay in Iraq until their contract is completed (Stillman, 2011a).

During interviews with Stillman (2011a), one of the women reported recurring physical and sexual abuse by one of her supervisors. Shortly after the reporter started conducting the interviews in early 2008, the women were repatriated after complaints were made about them making trouble on the base. Confronted with the allegations, a lawyer for Kulak stated that the company has never employed any individuals from Fiji and that Kulak "has a good reputation for sixty years" (Stillman, 2011a, para. 30).

3.4 Conclusion

This chapter has answered the first research question of this thesis on the extent to which KBR and their subcontractors are involved in TCN trafficking showing how TCNs are being lured into Iraq and revealing a long-standing and schematic system of TCN trafficking and labor abuses. The chapter illustrated that the practices of KBR and their subcontractors can in fact be considered crimes of human trafficking and forced labor as they fit into internationally recognized as well as US legal definitions of human trafficking and forced labor. Potentially, these crimes could even be deemed enslavement and thus a crime against humanity under Art. (7) (c) ICC Statute.

Chapter 4
Legal Framework

In the 2000s, shortly after reports had surfaced of USG contractors being involved in a sex-trafficking ring in Bosnia, human trafficking was adopted as a crime under the US law through the TVPA (Maffai, 2008). The Bosnia incident revealed striking shortcomings in US efforts to combat human trafficking and called for stricter actions and the assumption of jurisdiction for these crimes in US courts (ACLU & Yale Law School, 2012). However, even after the adoption of the TVPA, the government lacked adequate mechanisms to investigate and prosecute contractors for their involvement in human trafficking abroad. As private contractors are considered civilians rather than military personnel, they fell out of the scope of military jurisdiction. Furthermore, civilian courts lacked jurisdiction due to territorial limitations of the existing laws (Brown, 2007; ACLU & Yale Law School, 2012). When the DoD and other government agencies became more and more aware of these issues and their potential consequences for US missions abroad, the Bush administration implemented a "zero tolerance" policy against human trafficking as well as ongoing contractor impunity in 2002 and stipulated a series of reforms aiming at closing the jurisdictional gap likened to a legal "Bermuda Triangle" (Waits, 2006; ACLU & Yale Law School, 2012). Although these new reforms and legal amendments extended the scope of both military and the US criminal jurisdiction providing authorities with more power concerning the investigation and prosecution of contractors involved in human trafficking, "government agencies have failed to meaningfully implement or enforce them" (ACLU & Yale Law School, 2012, p. 43). Apparently, the willingness to properly deal with such cases is considerably low, and accountability still seems to only exist in theory, not in practice.

The following section will describe how the USG contractor KBR and their subcontractors are still able to engage in these crimes with impunity providing an overview of the existing legal tools that could potentially be applicable to cases of human trafficking and forced labor by the USG contractors. In this context, the Coalition Provisional Authority Order 17, the Uniform Code of Military Justice (UCMJ), the ATCA, the TVPA, and the Military Extraterritorial Jurisdiction Act

© The Author(s) 2018

C. Cole, R. Vermeltfoort, *U.S. Government Contractors and Human Trafficking*, SpringerBriefs in Criminology, https://doi.org/10.1007/978-3-319-70827-0_4

(MEJA) will be discussed. Furthermore, recent efforts by the USG to combat human trafficking will be briefly elucidated.

4.1 The Coalition Provisional Authority Order 17

In 2004, the head of the transitional government in Iraq, known as the Coalition Provisional Authority (CPA), issued the controversially debated Order 17 creating immunity from Iraqi law for a variety of actors in Iraq including USG prime contractors and subcontractors. The order states that "contractors shall not be subject to Iraqi laws or regulations in matters relating to their contract [and] shall be immune from Iraqi legal process" (CPA Order 17, 2004, p. 5). It further states that contractors shall only be subject to the laws of their sending countries meaning that the USG contractors shall only be subject to the US law.

In October 2007, shortly after the fatal Blackwater shooting in Baghdad that sparked considerable public outrage, the new Iraqi government approved a draft law that would revoke CPA Order 17 and thus contractors' immunity from Iraqi laws (BBC News, 2007). Subsequently, negotiations between the Iraqi and US governments on the issue of contractor immunity began, leading up to a 2008 US-Iraqi security agreement lifting immunity for foreign contractors (Tavernise, 2008). This means that from this time on, foreign contractors were subject to Iraqi law and could be tried in Iraqi courts for committed crimes. In 2011, the British national Daniel Fitzsimons was the first private contractor to be tried and given a prison sentence in an Iraqi court for the murder of two of his colleagues (Davies, 2011).

The revocation of CPA Order 17 is promising as it makes USG contractors subject to Iraqi laws. However, as concerns the crimes of human trafficking and forced labor, there has not yet been a case brought forward against a USG contractor in an Iraqi court.

4.2 The Uniform Code of Military Justice (UCMJ)

The UCMJ, dating back to 1951, is the criminal code on which the US court martial system is based. This military law was designed to regulate the conduct of the military and provided special military courts with jurisdiction over crimes committed by members of the armed forces (Waits, 2006). As initially the jurisdiction was strictly confined to military personnel, civilians, including civilian government contractors accompanying the military, usually fell out of the scope of the UCMJ. Civilians could only be subjected to UCMJ jurisdiction in the case of a war officially declared by the US Congress (ACLU & Yale Law School, 2012). However, in 2006, the Congress extended the UCMJ to specifically cover "persons serving with or accompanying an armed force in the field in time of declared war or contingency operations" (10 U.S.C. §802, Art. 2 (a) (10)). As the military operation on Iraq is deemed a contingency operation, the UCMJ could therefore potentially be applied to private contractors committing crimes during their employment in Iraq. However, the practical implication and impact of this UCMJ amendment remain unclear, as guidance concerning the implementation and reach is considered insufficient (ACLU & Yale Law School, 2012). Furthermore, scholars and legal experts argue that military courts will be extremely reluctant to make use of the amendment as "every extension of military jurisdiction is an encroachment on the jurisdiction of civil courts and, more important, acts as a deprivation of [...] treasured constitutional protections" (Reid v. Covert, 1956, p. 354). Therefore, the UCMJ remains to be a rather impotent legal instrument when it comes to prosecuting private contractors in Iraq for crimes of human trafficking and forced labor.

4.3 The Alien Tort Claims Act (ATCA)

Furthermore, the 1789 ATCA could provide trafficking victims and their families with a tool to sue government contractors for compensation in US district courts. The Act provides that "...the district courts shall have original jurisdiction of any civil action by an alien for a tort only, committed in violation of the law of nations or a treaty of the United States" (28 U.S.C. § 1350). Thus, in principle, the ATCA allows for civil action in the US district court in cases of violations of universally accepted international law standards irrespective of territorial considerations or the defendant and plaintiff's nationalities (Brown, 2007).

In 1980, the case of Filartiga v. Pena-Irala constituted the first case decided in the US Federal Court in which neither the plaintiff nor the defendant was a US citizen. This case is being considered as having created a new body of law "opening the door for foreign nationals to bring suit in the U.S. Federal Courts against individual violators of international law" (Brown, 2007, p. 758). In Filartiga v. Pena-Irala (1980), the court decided that the plaintiffs were to be awarded monetary compensation.

Another crucial case expanding the jurisdictional reach of the ATCA was Doe I v. Unocal in 2002. In this case the court decided that ATCA liability could be attached "individually to corporations for certain violations of international law" (Brown, 2007, p. 761) and furthermore significantly loosened the requirements for ATCA aiding and abetting liability.

However, in 2013, the decision in Kiobel et al. v. Royal Dutch Petroleum significantly restricted the reach of the ATCA stating that the case in question needs to have a "sufficient connection to the U.S." This decision was deemed a defeat for victims' rights and was harshly criticized by various human rights groups (Sriram, Ortega, & Herman, 2014).

As could be seen in Adhikari v. Daoud and Partners et al. (2014), US courts interpret the requirement "sufficient connection to the U.S." rather conservatively, and, therefore, this limitation of the ATCA has far-reaching implications for cases against USG contractors involving human trafficking and forced labor charges. In this case, the court, recalling the 2013 Kiobel decision, contended that there exists a "presumption against applying U.S. law outside U.S. territory" (Gillison, 2014, para. 21) and therefore dismissed all charges brought forward under the ATCA.

4.4 The Trafficking Victims Protection Act (TVPA)

The TVPA was adopted as a US law in 2000 and is considered the primary instrument for the USG to prosecute human trafficking offenses (Maffai, 2008). The TVPA explicitly criminalized human trafficking and forced labor and further required the Department of State (DoS) to monitor human trafficking worldwide and issue an annual report detailing its findings (Brown, 2007). Initially, the jurisdictional reach of the TVPA was confined to the US borders and thus did not provide for any extraterritorial application. However, in the 2005 and 2008 amendments to the Act, the Congress gradually introduced extraterritorial jurisdiction (Brown, 2007; ACLU & Yale Law School, 2012). The 2005 Trafficking Victims Protection Reauthorization Act (TVPRA) expanded the TVPA's reach to certain trafficking-related offenses committed by persons employed by or accompanying the USG outside the United States (TVPRA, 2005, § 2371). The 2005 TVPRA further underlined the need for stricter measures to guarantee accountability for USG contractors involved in human trafficking (ACLU & Yale Law School, 2012). In 2008, another TVPRA was passed, further expanding extraterritorial jurisdiction to all the crimes criminalized under the Act (Mattar, 2011). Simultaneously, the 2008 TVPRA restricted jurisdiction to US nationals, permanent residents, and persons otherwise present in the United States irrespective of nationality (TVPRA, 2008, § 223 (a)).

Evidently, the legislations introduced by the TVPRAs of 2005 and 2008 are promising tools in prosecuting private contractors for crimes of human trafficking and forced labor in Iraq. As the 2008 TVPRA restricted jurisdiction to US nationals, permanent residents, and persons present in the United States, it is particularly plausible that American prime contractors at the top of the recruitment chain, such as KBR, could be prosecuted under the present provisions. When it comes to subcontractors who are neither US based nor employ US nationals, the TVPRA would not hold up.

Since the TVPA and subsequent TVPRAs entered into force, only one lawsuit, the Daoud & Partners case, has been filed with regard to human trafficking and forced labor by USG contractors in Iraq. As mentioned above, this suit was finally dismissed because the alleged crimes had taken place in 2004 before the original TVPA was amended to provide extraterritorial application (see Adhikari v. Daoud & Partners et al., 2014).

4.5 The Military Extraterritorial Jurisdiction Act (MEJA)

Introduced in the 2000s, the same year the TVPA was passed, the Military Extraterritorial Jurisdiction Act (MEJA) entered into force as an additional response to the involvement of government contractors in serious crimes in the Balkans (Waits, 2006; Brown, 2007). The MEJA "amended federal [civilian] law to extend criminal jurisdiction to civilians, both U.S. citizens and foreign nationals, who commit criminal acts while employed by or accompanying the Armed Forces outside the

United States" (Waits, 2006, p. 516). Initially, the Act only covered individuals directly employed by the DoD but was amended in 2004 to include all contractors working in support of DoD missions, including subcontractors. MEJA applies to all crimes that would constitute a felony within the US territorial jurisdiction, including human trafficking (ACLU & Yale Law School, 2012).

Although the MEJA explicitly extended the jurisdiction of civilian courts to prosecute offenses by contractors regardless of nationality outside the United States, the Act shows several shortcomings obstructing its effective application in cases of USG contractors' involvement in human trafficking and forced labor. Firstly, the MEJA only applies to contractors who work for the support of DoD missions. Contractors working under the command of the DoS or other federal agencies fall outside the MEJA jurisdiction (ACLU & Yale Law School, 2012). Secondly, the MEJA "fails to mandate oversight and enforcement, [meaning that] even contractors who fall within its jurisdiction enjoy almost unlimited immunity for their actions" (ACLU & Yale Law School, 2012, p. 44). Solely the DoD Inspector General is responsible for referring cases to the US Attorney General for prosecution, and so far, not a single contractor has been prosecuted under the MEJA for human trafficking or forced labor in Iraq (ACLU & Yale Law School, 2012).

4.6 Recent Efforts by the USG to Fight Human Trafficking and Forced Labor

As elaborated above, the legal tools to prosecute USG contractors for human trafficking and forced labor remain considerably weak, and so far not a single contractor has been successfully prosecuted for these crimes. This sad fact however does not mean that the USG and especially the DoD ignore the problem of human trafficking by contractors—on the contrary, in recent years both President Obama and the DoD have addressed the issue multiple times acknowledging continuing challenges and insufficient action taken in this regard (DoD, 2014). In 2012, the President issued Executive Order (EO) 13627 entitled "Strengthening Protections Against Trafficking in Persons in Federal Contracts" calling for "stronger prohibitions on contractor engagement in human trafficking-related activities, new tailored compliance measures particularly in at-risk industries and sectors, and additional training in support of monitoring, identification, and compliance efforts" (DoD, 2014, p. 4). Furthermore, in 2013 the Congress passed an amendment to the National Defense Authorization Act on "Ending Trafficking in Government Contracting."

In 2014, the DoD published a comprehensive "Strategic Plan to Combat Trafficking in Persons" for the years 2014–2018, stating that the department is highly dedicated to eliminating human trafficking, labeling it a crime against humanity, and acknowledging that ongoing trafficking undermines the stability of US national security efforts at home and abroad (DoD, 2014). The plan consists of four goals emphasizing the importance of issuing DoD-wide policies to combat trafficking, partnering with internal and external stakeholders to coordinate prevention efforts, raising awareness through specialized training programs, and implementing standardized monitoring and enforcement procedures that enhance compliance and reporting (DoD, 2014).

These endeavors to combat human trafficking by government contractors by the President, Congress, and DoD are certainly a step in the right direction, and it is a welcomed development that the issue is being addressed more and more by government officials. However, it is highly questionable whether the recent efforts will effectively change the environment of impunity or will eventually lead to actual criminal prosecution of contractors who have been involved in human trafficking.

Although a big improvement, these measures by the USG do not provide for any new remedies for victims or tools to hold contractors accountable who have committed crimes of human trafficking and forced labor in the past. Of course, implementing new retroactively applicable laws and regulations in this regard would be more than questionable from a legal standpoint and is therefore entirely unrealistic. However, it would be in the USG's power to take serious action such as implementing new laws or amending the existing ones creating the realistic opportunity for contractors to be held criminally accountable for future cases of human trafficking and forced labor in Iraq or other warzones. Furthermore, effectively banning contractors like KBR from any future employment and terminating all existing contracts due to their involvement in these crimes would be feasible. This could certainly be an effective measure against future TCN trafficking and would prove that the USG is truly committed to the cause.

It is likely that efforts like EO 13627 and the 2014 DoD strategic plan will have an impact in the way that, for example, new zero-tolerance clauses on human trafficking will be implemented in future USG contracts or that DoD and contractor employees will receive mandatory anti-trafficking training. But one can reasonably question if these new and rather soft tools can effectively deter contractors from engaging in human trafficking and forced labor, especially when oversight regarding the compliance with contractors' contractual provisions has proven highly difficult to achieve. Therefore, only time will tell whether these new USG efforts will prove successful in actually combating human trafficking by contractors.

> Concluding, it is safe to say that actual accountability for these crimes committed by USG contractors remains to exist only in theory, not in practice. As Isenberg and Schwellenbach (2011) fittingly put it: "Is it really 'zero tolerance' when there are no [serious] repercussions?" (para. 81).

4.7 Conclusion

The above overview of the legal framework surrounding human trafficking and forced labor by USG contractors in Iraq as well as the recent efforts by the USG illustrate the complexity and legal uncertainty regarding this issue. Since 2008, USG contractors are subject to Iraqi law, opening up a new path for prosecuting

USG contractors for these crimes. However, Iraqi law has not yet been used in this regard. Under the US law, especially with regard to the MEJA and 2005/2008 TVPRAs, there certainly are promising legal tools to prosecute contractors for human trafficking and forced labor. However, as mentioned above, the willingness to investigate and prosecute has been remarkably low in the past. And even if new developments were to lead to an increased openness towards prosecuting contractors, legal scholars predict difficulties, mainly concerning the attribution of liability due to the extensive chain of subcontracting (Brown, 2007; ACLU & Yale Law School, 2012).

As a conclusion, one can contend that there exists a multitude of legal as well as policy documents dealing with both human trafficking and forced labor in general and USG contractors' involvement in those crimes. But as long as provisions and strategies only exist on paper and are not translated into mechanisms and actions to actually hold those contractors accountable who have committed serious crimes, the legal "Bermuda Triangle" in which they keep operating will not be closed. The chapter has illustrated that USG contractors like KBR and their subcontractors are able to keep engaging in human trafficking and forced labor with impunity as the existing legal tools and policies have so far proven useless for effectively prosecuting contractors for these crimes.

Chapter 5
Theoretical Framework

The past chapters of this thesis have depicted the emergence of the private military industry and answered the research questions as to what extent the USG contractor KBR and its subcontractors are involved in human trafficking and forced labor in Iraq and how these contractors are still able to engage in these crimes with impunity. The functional interdependency between private military contractors and the US government has been illustrated discussing their complex relationship and the unprecedented reliance on contract workers in Iraq without whom the entire mission would not have been possible (Singer, 2007). Such mutual interdependency between private and governmental entities has repeatedly stipulated the commission of illegal or injurious social action. This process and the development of crimes committed at the intersection of political and economic institutions is described and explained by state-corporate crime theory introduced by Kramer (1990a).

The present chapter will discuss how state-corporate crime theory can be applied to the subject of this thesis, namely, human trafficking and forced labor by KBR and its subcontractors in Iraq. Firstly, the initial concept of state-corporate crime by Kramer (1990a) will be explained, illustrating why the theory is suitable for this thesis. Secondly, the integrative theoretical model of state-corporate crime developed by Kramer and Michalowski (2006) to adequately analyze cases of state-corporate crime will be presented. The analysis in Chap. 6 of this thesis will subsequently apply state-corporate crime theory as well as the integrative model of state-corporate crime to answer the third research question of this thesis, namely, how the involvement of KBR and their subcontractors in the crimes of human trafficking and forced labor can be explained on criminological grounds.

© The Author(s) 2018

C. Cole, R. Vermeltfoort, *U.S. Government Contractors and Human Trafficking*,
SpringerBriefs in Criminology, https://doi.org/10.1007/978-3-319-70827-0_5

5.1 State-Corporate Crime

The concept of state-corporate crime was introduced by Kramer (1990a) in order to explain a form of crime characterized by the interplay of corporate crime and state crime—two distinct forms of white-collar crime. Clinard and Yeager (1980) define corporate crime as "…any act committed by corporations that is punished by the state, regardless of whether it is punished under administrative, civil or criminal law" (p. 16). State crime was originally defined by Chambliss (1989) as "acts defined by law as criminal and committed by state officials in the pursuit of their jobs as representatives of the state" (p. 183). This definition was further developed to include violations of international agreements, principles, and treaties. Thus, the concept of state crime not only refers to states' violations of their own national criminal law but also to the violation of international legal standards. This extension is deemed important, as states are unlikely to criminalize the social harms they commit (Soons, 2011).

In many cases of corporate involvement in international crimes or other gross human rights violations, it is difficult to determine whether the corporation or a state entity is the main perpetrator. There might be a strong degree of cooperation and shared interests of corporations and states that lead to the commission of serious crimes (Huisman, 2010). Accordingly, Kramer combined the two concepts of corporate crime and state crime defining state-corporate crime as:

> …an illegal or socially injurious action that is the collective product of the interaction between a business corporation and a state agency engaged in a joint endeavor. These crimes involve the active participation of two or more organizations, at least one of which is private and one of which is public. They are the harmful result of an inter-organizational relationship between business and government (Kramer, 1990a, p. 1).

The concept of state-corporate crime was further developed distinguishing between two forms of deviant inter-organizational relationships that can serve as the basis for state-corporate crime—namely, state-initiated corporate crime and state-facilitated corporate crime. Kramer and Michalowski (2006) describe state-initiated corporate crime as a situation where "corporations, employed by the government, engage in organizational deviance at the direction of, or with […] approval of, the government" (p. 21). On the other hand, the authors define state-facilitated corporate crime as a situation where "government institutions of social control are guilty of clear failure to create regulatory institutions capable of restraining deviant business activities, either because of direct collusion between business and government or because they adhere to shared goals whose attainment would be hampered by aggressive regulation" (p. 21).

The concept of state-corporate crime seems well suited for an analysis of KBR and their subcontractors' involvement in human trafficking and forced labor. Evidently, there exists an inter-organizational relationship between business/private entities, namely, KBR in Iraq, and a government/public entity, namely, the USG. There is a direct link between the USG and KBR, as the contractor is being awarded lucrative government contracts to provide logistical services on military bases in Iraq. The two entities therefore find themselves in a typical seller-buyer situation and have formed a close inter-organizational relationship. Therefore, the concept of state-corporate crime will be used for the analysis of this thesis.

5.2 The Integrative Model of State-Corporate Crime

On the basis of Kramer's (1990a) concept of state-corporate crime, Kramer and Michalowski (2006) proposed an integrative theoretical model of state-corporate crime that can be utilized to analyze such cases. The aim of the authors was to create a framework able to depict the complex interconnections and interdependences of corporations and state actors on a vertical and horizontal level in order to holistically examine cases of state-corporate crime. The model integrates the three major theoretical approaches to the study of corporate criminal behavior, each focusing on different levels of analysis. Firstly, differential association theory introduced by Sutherland (1949) proposes a rather micro-level social psychological approach to corporate crime focusing on individual learning processes that eventually lead to deviant behavior (Kramer & Michalowski, 2006). This approach, while having delivered valuable insights for criminological analysis, was criticized by many authors warning that focusing only on processes within an individual leads to an underestimation of the influence of organizational and institutional dynamics on the commission of crimes.

As a result of this criticism, various theoretical approaches emerged concentrating on organizational characteristics of corporate and governmental crime (see Albanese, 1982a; Clinard & Yeager, 1980; Gross, 1978; Coleman, 1987). This organizational perspective is characterized by the assumption that the structure of and dynamics within an organization are the main factors inducing the engagement in deviant behavior (Gross, 1978). The most prominent approach within the organizational perspective is Coleman's (1987) *rational-choice, blocked opportunity model*, stating that "organizations break the law because they are blocked in some fashion from access to legitimate means to achieve organizational goals" (Kramer & Michalowski, 2006, p. 22). Furthermore, Hopkins (1978) proposed an approach focusing on internal structures and defective standard operating procedures of the organization.

The political-economic perspective is the third school of thought incorporated in the integrative model on state-corporate crime (see Barnett, 1981; Chambliss, 1989; Michalowski & Kramer, 1987; Young, 1981). The political-economic perspective has many similarities with the organizational perspective depicted above as both perspectives focus on the organization as their primary subject of analysis (Kauzlarich and Kramer, 1998a). However, the political-economic perspective not so much concentrates on the structure and dynamics within organizations but rather focuses on constraints on organizations by markets and states in a broader economic context. According to Barnett (1981), deviant corporate behavior will occur "when management chooses to pursue corporate goals through circumvention of market constraints in a manner prohibited by the state" (p. 5). Furthermore, profit maximization and private accumulation are deemed crucial factors by some authors explaining corporate crime (Young, 1981). These factors can also contribute to crimes by governments aiming at optimizing the conditions for the operation of their transnational corporations (Kauzlarich and Kramer, 1998b). Kramer and Michalowski (2006) furthermore contend that governmental deviance can stem from the complexity of institutional structures of most modern states. The authors explain this assumption by stating that conflicting goals of different government units can lead to one of those units blocking the attainment of organizational goals by the other unit leading to the blocked unit experiencing pressure towards deviant strategies to pursue their goals.

Kramer and Michalowski (2006) argue that corporate as well as governmental crime can best be explained when the divergent approaches discussed above are integrated into a multidimensional framework focusing on the interplay of micro, meso, and macro factors. This integration of micro, meso, and macro approaches allows for a holistic study of cases on the (1) individual, (2) organizational, and (3) institutional level. The authors furthermore assert that corporate criminal behavior is the outcome of a "coincidence of pressure for goal attainment, availability and attractiveness of illegitimate means and an absence of effective social control" (p. 24). Thus, Kramer and Michalowski (2006) identified three interdependent so-called *catalysts for action* applicable to each level of analysis: (1) motivation, (2) opportunity, and (3) control. The proposed model links the three levels of analysis with the three identified catalysts for action and therefore offers a useful multidimensional approach to explain cases of state-corporate crime.

Chapter 6
Analysis

In the subsequent chapter, the involvement of KBR and its subcontractors in human trafficking and forced labor in Iraq will be analyzed along the lines of the integrative model of state-corporate crime. This analysis aims at depicting how the complex functional interdependency between institutional and organizational actors, namely, the USG and KBR in Iraq, contributed to the commission of serious cases of human trafficking and forced labor. Firstly, I will focus on *motivations*, the first catalyst for action identified by Kramer and Michalowski (2006). As we have seen above, *motivations* in the integrative model of state-corporate crime refer to the motivations for the committed crimes. However, for answering the particular research question of this thesis, not only the motivations of KBR for the commission of the crimes of human trafficking and forced labor are relevant but also the motivations of the USG to employ PMCs in Iraq to such a large extent in the first place. The motivation and strong incentives for the USG to employ PMCs leading to a total reliance and interdependency between the USG and these contractors paved the way for the subsequent commission of crimes. Therefore it is crucial to firstly discuss the USG's motivations for the employment of PMCs in Iraq. Subsequently, KBR's and its subcontractors' motivations concerning the commission of the crimes of human trafficking and forced labor will be analyzed before similarly going about with the second catalyst for action, *opportunities*. As is the case with *motivations*, the opportunities on the side of the USG to award contracts to KBR in Iraq are an important factor leading up to the commission of crimes and will therefore be elaborated in addition to KBR's opportunities for perpetrating these crimes. Lastly, the third catalyst for action, *control*, will be analyzed depicting both controls on prime contractors like KBR as well as on subcontractors concerning the crimes in question.

© The Author(s) 2018

C. Cole, R. Vermeltfoort, *U.S. Government Contractors and Human Trafficking*, SpringerBriefs in Criminology, https://doi.org/10.1007/978-3-319-70827-0_6

6.1 Motivations

6.1.1 Motivations for Contracts

The motivations on the side of the USG to utilize private contractors in Iraq to such a large and unprecedented extent were mostly of a political and tactical nature (Singer, 2007). As briefly mentioned in Sect. 2.4 of this thesis, by utilizing private contractors, the USG was aiming at avoiding public dissent concerning the military mission in Iraq. After the devastating death tolls and massive public outrage during and after the Vietnam War (1955–1975), it became the aim of US military leaders to "preserve the tie between the nation's foreign policy decisions and local communities [by ensuring] that the military would not go to war without the sufficient backing [...] of the nation" (Singer, 2007, p. 2). These principles were enshrined in the so-called "Abrams Doctrine," named after then Army Chief of Staff General Creighton Abrams.

The Bush administration therefore reasoned that sending a relatively low number of actual US troops to Iraq and in turn increasingly relying on private contractors to carry out tasks initially provided by the military would lead to greater public support for the mission (Rothe, 2006; Singer, 2007). Thus, from the beginning of the military mission to Iraq, vast numbers of private contractors were deployed to the warzone, and at times these contractors even outnumbered the actual US troops on the ground (see Schwartz and Swain, 2011). Throughout the Iraq occupation up until to the point where the Obama administration started to plan the US withdrawal from the country in 2007, the number of contractors steadily grew. Singer (2007) contends that this development was sparked by the realization on the side of the Bush administration that the 135,000 initially deployed troops were insufficient to successfully carry out the mission in Iraq. But instead of sending more regular forces and thus publicly admitting that the planning of the operation was flawed concerning the required resources, a politically highly undesirable endeavor, more and more private contractors were sent to the warzone (Singer, 2007).

The key motivational factor that makes the deployment of vast numbers of private contractors so desirable for the USG is most likely the fact that the American public remains unaware of the considerable number of contractors in Iraq. When it comes to the deployment of actual US troops, the USG has to officially declare the number of uniformed personnel that are being sent to warzones. This is not the case with private contractors (Singer, 2007). Furthermore, private contractor casualties are not reported or tallied in official statistics on military deaths, as the employees of contractors count as civilians rather than military personnel (Rothe, 2006; Li, 2015). As officially published military death tolls usually have a significant impact on public support for a mission, leaving contractor deaths out of the tally, and therefore being able to keep the official death toll of the Iraq war relatively low was a highly attractive prospect for the USG (Singer, 2007). Singer contends that the "public didn't even hear about contactor losses, and when they did, they had far less blowback on our government" (p. 4). Furthermore, Singer (2007) illustrates the considerable discrepancy in official death tolls versus actual losses including both soldiers and private contractors by stating that "the private military industry has suffered more losses in Iraq than the rest of the coalition of allied nations combined" (p. 4). Thus, by resorting to private contractors to such a considerable extent and leaving the American public largely unaware of this development, the USG has endeavored to save the direct political costs of the military mission to Iraq, namely, to lose the backing and support of the majority of the American population (Singer, 2007; Rothe, 2006). Furthermore, the argument brought forward that utilizing private corporations in warzones is more cost-effective than the military and that this practice would therefore save citizens' tax money (Rothe, 2006). Rothe (2006) further argues that the lack of accountability of private military contractors under international criminal law and other legal instruments could be an incentive for the USG to hire these companies.

Considering all the abovementioned points, the motivations of the USG to award contracts to PMCs in Iraq become evident.

On the side of KBR, the motivation to obtain government contracts was clearly profit driven. The USG's aim to outsource considerable amounts of military work to private contractors has created a multibillion dollar business for a large array of companies, including logistic providers such as KBR, wishing to obtain lucrative contracts in Iraq (Rothe, 2006; Singer, 2007). This goal of making maximum profit has in the past resulted in several cases of fraudulent war profiteering in Iraq involving Halliburton and KBR. The company was repeatedly accused of overcharging the USG for its services by reporting sums of money allegedly spent for commodities that in reality far exceeded the company's actual expenses (Rothe, 2006; ACLU & Yale Law School, 2012). This way, KBR, which was at times struggling with declining stock values and regaining previously suffered monetary losses, found a way to make maximum profits in Iraq (Rothe, 2006).

6.1.2 Motivations for Crimes

KBRs and their subcontractors' motivation to become involved in TCN trafficking and forced labor can be explained by similar profit-driven reasons. As KBR and its former mother company Halliburton already have a history of fraudulent practices including bribery, corruption, and serious cases of war profiteering, it is not surprising that the company eventually engaged in these crimes once their lucrativeness was discovered.

According to the ACLU & Yale Law School, (2012), prime contractors as well as subcontractors are able to make enormous profits from engaging in trafficking and labor abuses of TCNs on military bases. There are two major areas where contractors are able to profit from the commission of these crimes, namely, the routine underpayment of TCNs and the kickbacks from illegal recruitment fees charged to TCNs (ACLU & Yale Law School, 2012). As elaborated in Sect. 3.2.2 on the recruiting process of TCNs, recruited workers in Iraq regularly only earn a fraction of what has been promised to them during the recruitment in their countries of origin. It is estimated that contractors bill the government an annual rate of $67,600 per full-time TCN. However, salaries awarded to TCNs are typically as low as $1800–6000 per year, leaving the contractor with an exorbitantly high profit per hired worker (ACLU & Yale Law School, 2012; Li, 2015). It could be argued that contractors spend a significant amount of money to pay indirect contract costs for transport, food, and accommodation of TCNs, which would allow for a certain discrepancy in TCN salaries and the amount charged to the USG. However, all the evidence presented throughout this thesis speak against this argument, and even if contractors would spend "lavishly on food and accommodation for TCNs […] the total cost per TCN would still come nowhere close to $67,600" (ACLU & Yale Law School, 2012, p. 27). Thus, it is likely that KBR and the company's subcontractors, by underpaying TCNs, make up to ten times the profit they would make if TCNs were paid the whole amount the USG pays for their employment.

Furthermore, contractors profit from the illegal recruitment fees that TCNs pay the local recruitment agents. According to Kavinnamannil and McCahon (2011), contractors usually receive 50% of these fees, estimating a total profit of $312 million from recruitment fee kickbacks so far gained by contractors.[1]

Concluding the elucidated dynamics and considering KBR's shady history of fraudulent practices and war profiteering, the company's involvement in human trafficking and labor abuses can be regarded as part of a broader system of contractor malfeasance driven by the motivation to make maximum profits.

6.2 Opportunities

Motivation alone does not suffice, however, to explain why these crimes could occur and can continue without effective accountability. Therefore, *opportunity*, the second catalyst for action identified by Kramer and Michalowski (2006), will be taken into consideration in the following section.

[1] See ACLU, 2012, p. 28 for a hypothetical fraudulent contractor recruitment scenario including estimated amounts of money earned by prime contractor, subcontractor, recruitment agent, and TCN.

6.2.1 Opportunities for Contracts

In addition to the motivation of the USG to hire PMCs like KBR in Iraq, there must exist the opportunity to award contracts to these companies. Furthermore, there must be the opportunity for the company to obtain government contracts (Rothe, 2006). In the case of KBR in Iraq, these opportunities were mainly created by regulatory changes implemented by the Bush administration and the fact that VP Dick Cheney had previously headed the company Halliburton, KBR's former mother company.

In April 2001, shortly after George W. Bush and Dick Cheney took office, the administration paved the way for KBR to obtain government contracts by revoking a regulation previously implemented by the Clinton administration that aimed at regulating companies holding or obtaining government contracts (Rothe, 2006). This regulation 65 FR 80255 provided for a careful background check of companies regarding their business record, past felony, or civil charges against the company as well as the company's record of integrity and business ethics. Companies were required to have a satisfactory record of "compliance with the law, including tax, labor, employment, environment, antitrust and consumer protection laws" (Rothe, 2006, p. 232). It is safe to argue that with Halliburton and KBR's dubious legal history, they would not have qualified for contracts under the Clinton regulation. Therefore, by revoking this rule, the Bush administration created the opportunity for KBR to be hired as a USG contractor in Iraq.

Furthermore and most obviously, the military mission to Iraq in itself and the subsequent occupation of the country created the opportunity for PMCs to be hired by the USG. As contended by Rothe (2006), the opportunity for companies like KBR providing logistical services in warzones was further reinforced by a Bush administration ruling that "…no Iraqi state-owned companies would be eligible to bid for reconstruction contracts" (p. 233). This meant that although it would have most probably been more cost-effective and would have given employment to thousands of Iraqi individuals, the administration opted to hand out all contracts for logistics, reconstruction, transport, and base support services to US contractors and mainly to KBR. Apart from these questionable rules and regulations implemented by the Bush administration, the fact that contracts were awarded to KBR to such a large extent, providing the company with billions of dollars of profit is in itself highly suspicious when considering the close connection of Dick Cheney to the company. Being the VP and former CEO of Halliburton, Cheney clearly found himself in a legally dubious conflict of interest that provided Halliburton subsidiary KBR with favorable positions and a level of access to contracts that no other company enjoyed to this extent (Rothe, 2006; Young, 2013).

6.2.2 *Opportunities for Crimes*

On the side of KBR, one can contend that the so-called "*cost-plus*" nature of the company's contracts with the USG provided them with an opportunity to overcharge the government for their services and thus allows the company to enormously profit from their involvement in the crimes of trafficking and forced labor (Brown, 2007; Rothe, 2006). Cost-plus contracts are defined as agreements "to pay a company for a job based on the amount of money used to buy the materials required to complete that job" (Investopedia, n.d., para.1).[2] That means that companies are being fully reimbursed for all expenses they have for fulfilling their contractual duties. In the case of KBR in Iraq, that means that the company was easily able to charge the government more money for their services than they actually required. This technique allowed for KBR and their subcontractors to profit enormously from TCN trafficking and labor abuses on military bases (Chatterjee 2010; ACLU & Yale Law School, 2012; Rothe, 2006). As mentioned above, the amount of money the contractors charge the government for an annual salary of one TCN is up to ten times higher than what the workers are actually paid. Furthermore it is reported that housing costs are also fraudulently billed (ACLU & Yale Law School, 2012). Without these cost-plus contracts, overcharging would be a lot harder for contractors, making their involvement in a wide array of crimes including human trafficking and forced labor a lot less lucrative and attractive.

Having considered the abovementioned factors, it is evident that the opportunity on the side of the USG is given to hire KBR as well as the opportunity for KBR to attain government contracts and to subsequently profit from the commission of crimes due to the nature of cost-plus contracts.

6.3 Control

The absence of effective controls and constraints on prime contractors, like KBR and its subcontractors, further facilitated the contractors' malfeasance and commission of crimes. The next paragraph will therefore analyze the third catalyst for action: *control.*

6.3.1 *Control on Prime Contractors*

The striking lack of effective control mechanisms regarding private contractors being involved in cases of TCN trafficking and forced labor in Iraq has already been demonstrated in Sect. 3.4 above, describing the legal framework surrounding

[2] With regard to the duties of KBR in Iraq, "materials required to complete the job" are, for example, trucks for transporting goods and personnel, construction materials, and food, but also the workers required to run the military bases.

private contractors and their commission of crimes. It has become evident that private military contractors overseas are operating in a legal vacuum and that the existing laws are insufficiently applied in respect to the investigation and prosecution of TCN trafficking and forced labor by PMCs. Neither the application of the UCMJ, ATCA, or TVPRA nor the MEJA has led to any successful legal cases against a private contractor for their involvement in human trafficking or forced labor. Furthermore, up until 2008, the possibility to hold KBR and their subcontractors accountable for human trafficking and forced labor allegations under Iraqi law was diminished by CPA Order 17 exempting contractors from being subject to Iraqi laws in the course of their official activities (Brown, 2007; Rothe, 2006; ACLU & Yale Law School, 2012). This means that private contractors were systematically protected from being held legally accountable for their actions. Having been able to operate in a more or less lawless environment without adequate legal tools and regulations controlling their conduct or deterring the development of deviant patterns of operation, PMCs have been "relatively free to behave as they see fit" (Rothe, 2006).

But not only the lack of legal accountability in this regard is striking, internal DoD controls on contractors are also remarkably weak which is mainly due to a considerable downsizing of initially 7030 to only 3958 workers in the DoD's defense contract audit agency during the 1990s (Rothe, 2006). This led to poor auditing and oversight of the rapidly increasing number of government contracts once the intervention in Iraq had started. Subsequent congressional initiatives to introduce more effective monitoring and regulations were rigorously dismissed by the administration stating that they "...don't agree oversight is necessary" (Rothe, 2006, p. 234). The scarce controls that were in place, like the 2003 audit of Halliburton revealing cases of overcharging and fraud, were furthermore strictly ignored by the administration continuing to award lucrative contracts to Halliburton and its subsidiaries (Rothe, 2006).

In 2003, the Bush administration furthermore started to outsource a major part of the auditing work to private companies to compensate for the declined number of employees (Rothe, 2006; Bauman, Reid, & McDermid, 2011). In practice, that means that now private contractors were in charge of monitoring and overseeing the work of other private contractors who could likely be potential business partners. The effectiveness of these oversight practices can therefore be legitimately doubted.

6.3.2 Control on Subcontractors

Furthermore, the chain of extensive subcontracting further obstructs effective control and oversight. It has been repeatedly criticized by journalists and scholars how little information the USG actually has on the operation of Middle Eastern subcontractors, and that sometimes it is even unclear to the USG who is hired by prime contractors and thus who they are eventually paying (Isenberg, 2012; Tyler, 2012). It is estimated that approximately 70% of prime contractors' work is being outsourced to subcontractors, and, yet, there is no adequate system in place for the DoD and other USG agencies to track how much money is paid to these subcontractors or in what kind of activities they engage (Tyler, 2012). The USG apparently tries to gain oversight on contractors through the so-called flow-down provisions which are to be included in prime contractors' contracts with subcontractors (Isenberg, 2012). These provisions state that the subcontractors shall have the same obligations to the USG as the prime contractors, which should lead to the possibility of stronger oversight, reporting, and transparency on subcontractors' operations. However, it has been reported that prime contractors regularly fail to effectively implement and subsequently monitor subcontractors' compliance with these provisions. This system of uncertainty, lack of reporting, and insufficient information on subcontractors' activities can easily lead to patterns of criminal or injurious social behavior (Isenberg, 2012).

Concerning KBR and their subcontractors in Iraq and other Middle Eastern nations, this illustrates that the USG does not have the means to sufficiently oversee subcontractors' criminal activities and to consequently hold them accountable for their involvement in human trafficking and forced labor. Subcontractors like Daoud, Najlaa, and Kulak can still engage in these practices and eventually are being paid for their services with money provided by the USG.

On the side of KBR, the company has consistently stated that it ensures "that all subcontractors are in compliance with both the U.S. government and KBR Code of Business Conduct" (Isenberg & Schwellenbach, 2011, para. 43). After the Najlaa incident in 2008, revealing intolerable living conditions and allegations of labor abuses at man camps run by the Kuwaiti subcontractor, KBR reportedly launched an investigation into the situation (Isenberg, 2012; Isenberg & Schwellenbach, 2011). After stating that the situation at the Najlaa-run camp constitutes a "corporate embarrassment" for KBR, the company threatened to terminate some of the contracts previously awarded to the subcontractor. An email conversation disclosed to the Project on Government Oversight (POGO) in 2011 revealed that KBR feared repercussions from the USG due to the widely publicized incident stating that the USG "is extremely upset at KBR right now and most of that frustration comes from Najlaa" (Isenberg & Schwellenbach, 2011, para. 38). However, upon further investigations and requests for information by POGO in 2009 as to the consequences of the incident, KBR simply replied that "Najlaa responded without delay to KBR's demand for corrective action, and the matter was resolved appropriately. [The company continues] to work with Najlaa and other subcontractors today in providing much needed services to our troops" (Isenberg & Schwellenbach, 2011, para. 78).

The abovementioned facts illustrate that although KBR claims to ensure its subcontractors' compliance with USG codes of conduct and showed some efforts to investigate the Najlaa incident, the company's efforts have certainly not been adequate to reach effective oversight and control as no serious consequences were implemented after this grave incident.

Concluding the abovementioned facts, one can safely argue that in addition to the insufficient legal instruments surrounding TCN trafficking and forced labor by USG contractors, there exists a lack of control and internal oversight by the USG on both prime contractors and subcontractors. Furthermore, as illustrated by KBR's reaction to the Najlaa incident, prime contractor KBR is failing at adequately controlling its subcontractors and keeping up to its promise of ensuring subcontractors' compliance with USG rules and regulations. These insufficient controls provide contractors with unlimited opportunities to engage in criminal behavior such as human trafficking and forced labor, as they could be sure that their behavior goes unpunished.

Chapter 7
Summary and Conclusions

The aim of this thesis has been to answer the research questions as presented in Chap. 1:

To what extent is the USG contractor KBR and their subcontractors involved in human trafficking and forced labor of TCNs in Iraq?
How are these contractors still able to engage in these crimes with impunity?
How can the involvement in human trafficking and forced labor by these contractors be explained criminologically?

In order to provide contextual background information on PMCs, Chap. 2 of this thesis illustrated the history and dynamics of the private military industry in general, before elucidating the role of PMCs, especially KBR, in the US-occupied Iraq. We have learned that the vast utilization of PMCs in Iraq has been unprecedented in comparison with previous wars. Furthermore, the undesired implications and consequences of PMCs operating in Iraq and the insufficient planning regarding their increased deployment have been discussed.

Subsequently, Chap. 3 elucidated the extent to which KBR and their subcontractors are involved in the crimes of human trafficking and forced labor in Iraq answering the first research questions of this thesis. We have learned who TCNs are, how they are being recruited and trafficked to US military bases in Iraq, and what kind of abusive living and working conditions TCNs are being subjected to during their time in Iraqi man camps run by KBR subcontractors. The chain of actors involved in the recruitment process including prime contractors, subcontractors, recruitment agents, and loan sharks has been described illustrating the complexity and obscurity of the situation. Furthermore, it became clear throughout the chapter that the described practices and depicted cases involving KBR and their subcontractors fall under internationally recognized as well as US legal definitions of human trafficking and forced labor. Thus, one can conclude that KBR and their subcontractors violate both international anti-trafficking and the US law by engaging in the systematic exploitation, trafficking, and forced labor of TCNs in Iraq. The committed

© The Author(s) 2018

C. Cole, R. Vermeltfoort, *U.S. Government Contractors and Human Trafficking*, SpringerBriefs in Criminology, https://doi.org/10.1007/978-3-319-70827-0_7

crimes could even be considered crimes against humanity under the provision on enslavement, Art. (7) (1) (c), of the ICC Statute.

Chapter 4 introduced the legal framework surrounding the crimes of human trafficking and forced labor by USG government contractors and subcontractors in order to answer the second research question of this thesis, namely, why these contractors are still able to commit these grave crimes with impunity. The chapter provided a comprehensive overview of the US legal framework surrounding the crimes of human trafficking and forced labor and the possibilities for prosecution of private contractors like KBR and their subcontractors in Iraq. We have learned that there exist a number of promising legal tools concerning this matter but that sadly the USG has so far failed to meaningfully implement and enforce them resulting in the impunity of USG contractors and subcontractors for the crimes of human trafficking and forced labor.

Following the rather descriptive first chapters of this thesis, Chaps. 5 and 6 were dedicated to answering the third research question and thus analyzing how KBR and their subcontractors' involvement in human trafficking and forced labor can be explained criminologically. For this purpose, the theory of state-corporate crime by Kramer (1990a) and the integrative model of state-corporate crime by Kramer and Michalowski (2006) were utilized. The three catalysts for action identified by Kramer and Michalowski (2006), (1) *motivation*, (2) *opportunity*, and (3) *control*, were each analyzed with respect to KBR as well as the USG in order to illustrate the complex interplay of explanatory factors contributing to the commission of the crimes of human trafficking and forced labor by KBR and their subcontractors.

Firstly, while analyzing the motivations of the USG to employ a large number of PMCs in Iraq, we have learned that this decision was highly politically motivated. There are strong political incentives for the USG to utilize private contractors for supporting their military missions overseas. Smaller numbers of uniformed personnel and thus less official military casualties leading to a desired increase in public acceptance for warfare is clearly one of the strongest motivational factors. The motivation on the side of KBR to be hired by the USG for services in Iraq was clearly to make maximum profit. The war in Iraq was a unique opportunity for private contractors to obtain lucrative business contracts, and KBR was hoping for a piece of the cake. The motivation for KBR to subsequently become involved in human trafficking and forced labor of TCNs is also connected to the profit-driven nature of the company. As we have seen throughout this thesis, trafficking and labor abuses constitute a lucrative business for the company and their subcontractors, as they are able to generate profits from recruitment fee kickbacks and by significantly underpaying their workers.

The opportunities for the USG to award contracts to KBR were mainly created by questionable regulatory changes by the Bush administration and Dick Cheney's legally and morally dubious relationship with KBR's former mother company Halliburton, paving the way for KBR to be employed in Iraq. The cost-plus nature of KBR's contracts with the USG enabling the contractor to charge the USG a multiple of the amount that they actually pay TCNs furthermore enabled KBR to make maximum profits from engaging in TCN trafficking.

Insufficient legal accountability, control, and oversight additionally contribute to KBR and their subcontractors' engagement in an ongoing impunity for these crimes. As we have learned, controls and oversight on both prime contractors and subcontractors are considerably weak and poorly enforced by the USG. Their ongoing operation in a legal "Bermuda Triangle" allows contractors to engage in criminal activities without serious repercussions.

After having analyzed all these factors on the organizational (KBR) as well as on the institutional level (USG), we can contend that the involvement of USG contractor KBR and their subcontractors in human trafficking in Iraq is a clear case of state-corporate crime as defined by Kramer (1990a). The intertwining motivations as well as the opportunity structure and lack of adequate controls elucidated above illustrate that the crimes in question are a collective product of the close interaction between and the mutual interests of a business entity, namely, KBR and a political entity, namely, the USG. As regards the distinction between state-initiated and state-facilitated corporate crime, the USG can be considered a facilitator of KBR and their subcontractors' perpetration of crimes, as the USG is "guilty of clear failure to create regulatory institutions capable of restraining deviant business activities" (Kramer & Michalowski, 2006, p. 21).

As long as the USG fails to take appropriate action through internal and external control mechanisms, effective oversight, and monitoring as well as functioning legal instruments to regulate private contractors' activities, the trafficking and forced labor of TCNs in Iraq are likely to continue with impunity for contractors like KBR and their subcontractors and devastating consequences for the victims.

Chapter 8
Discussion

The last chapter of this thesis will be dedicated to critically reviewing the conducted research and proposing some suggestions for potential further research on the topic.

Firstly, it is crucial to note that the conducted research is largely based on journalistic sources. Although there exist some scholarly works on the topic of TCN trafficking by USG contractors, these articles are still scarce, and, therefore, reliance on journalistic sources and NGO reports was inevitable for writing this thesis. Especially the information used to write Sects. 3.2 and 3.3 on the situation of TCNs in Iraq and well-documented cases of TCN trafficking by KBR subcontractors heavily rely on such pieces. The reliability and accuracy of these sources can be viewed critically from a methodological standpoint, as the information provided in journalistic sources is sometimes poorly substantiated, speculative, or exaggerated in order to gain public attention. In order to prevent the reliance on such flawed information in this thesis, the facts provided by the used sources were meticulously examined as well as thoroughly and critically reviewed. Triangulation was used, taking into account and carefully comparing various sources reporting on the same incidents to ensure the accuracy of the provided information.

Furthermore, one can critically remark that the analytical part of this thesis solely focuses on motivations, opportunities, and control on the organizational and institutional level as the catalysts for action were only depicted for KBR as a company and the USG as an institutional/political entity. The absence of a micro-level analysis examining motivations, opportunities, and control on an individual level is due to a lack of information concerning individual actors within the company from which one could derive explanatory factors for the commission of the crimes of TCN trafficking and forced labor. Obtaining such information and therefore being able to analyze how and why individual employees of KBR and their subcontractors engage in these crimes would require further empirical research preferably in the form of interviews with implicated (former) employees. While conducting such research seems feasible, it would definitely involve difficulties locating individuals who are willing to talk about such sensitive issues. Furthermore, conducting research in a

© The Author(s) 2018

C. Cole, R. Vermeltfoort, *U.S. Government Contractors and Human Trafficking*,
SpringerBriefs in Criminology, https://doi.org/10.1007/978-3-319-70827-0_8

(post) conflict society like Iraq as well as countries like Kuwait or United Arab Emirates poses challenges as to security matters and cultural barriers.

In addition to the suggestion for further research mentioned above, one needs to continuously monitor and observe new developments concerning oversight and legal accountability of PMCs for their involvement in the crimes of human trafficking and forced labor. As we have seen throughout this thesis, the tools in place remain considerably weak. However, as described in Sect. 4.5, more and more efforts are being made on the side of the USG to combat these crimes, and it will prove highly interesting as to whether and how these new policies will be translated into concrete actions.

Concluding the conducted research, one can contend that this thesis has provided valuable insights and explanations not only concerning the crimes of human trafficking and forced labor by KBR and their subcontractors. Case studies are usually aiming at understanding the dynamics of the particular incident in question and not at finding generalizable explanations for a variety of cases. However, the explanations provided in the analysis of this thesis could potentially be transferred to other profit-driven crimes committed by PMCs in warzones. The opportunity structure in place, namely, the cost-plus contracts awarded to contractors like KBR by the USG allows these profit-driven contractors to overcharge the USG significantly for TCN salaries paying them only a fraction of what they are being reimbursed for. One could argue that the same pattern of motivation to make maximum profit combined with cost-plus contracts and a lack of effective control and oversight on contractors could be applied to other crimes committed by PMCs that are directed at making maximum profit such as overcharging for food supplies and the transport of goods (Rothe, 2006).

When trying to further generalize the explanations provided in this thesis to other crimes by PMCs such as the prominent Blackwater shootings or the Abu Ghraib torture scandal, one encounters difficulties with regard to the motivations and opportunities for the crimes. Evidently, the underlying motivation of every contractor employed in Iraq is to make profit. However, it is highly questionable whether the particular crimes committed by the contractors in these particular incidents were as clearly profit-driven, as is the case with TCN trafficking and forced labor by KBR and their subcontractors. Furthermore, the opportunity structures enabling the commission of the crimes in the different cases vary largely. The nature of the cost-plus contracts is considered the main factor creating opportunity for KBR and their subcontractors to commit crimes, whereas, for example, in the Abu Ghraib scandal, ineffective prison management, conflicting orders, and a lack of division of labor constituted the crucial factors establishing the opportunity for the torture and abuse to occur (Soons, 2011).

But as regards control, our third catalyst of action, one can validly argue that the lack of control mechanisms on contractors contributes not only to the commission of the clearly profit-driven crimes by KBR but also to other PMCs perpetrating other types of crimes. There exists a general lack of adequate oversight and control on PMCs' (criminal) activities, and as long as the USG does not succeed in implementing effective legal regulation and monitoring on all PMCs employed in warzones, the commission of serious crimes by PMCs is unlikely to cease.

Concluding one can say that the explanations and insights provided in this thesis could potentially be used as indicators for the analysis of future crimes committed by PMCs, especially if these crimes are profit-driven and perpetrated by PMCs operating under cost-plus contracts.

Part II
From Peacekeepers to Perpetrators: Case Study of Private Contractor DynCorp and Their Complicity in Sex Trafficking in Post-War Bosnia

Chapter 9
Introduction

On December 14, 1995, 4 years of brutal war in Bosnia came to an end when the parties to the conflict signed the Dayton Peace Agreement in Paris. In accordance with the agreement, an International Police Task Force (hereinafter IPTF) was created, consisting of international police, civilian contractors, and international peacekeepers. As part of the IPTF, the private military company DynCorp went to Bosnia with the task to advise and monitor the local Bosnian police, especially on human rights. They were sent as peacekeepers, but as time progressed a vast group of DynCorp employees became involved in brutal sex trafficking of underage girls. This thesis tries to unravel how those peacekeepers designated to protect human rights, in fact, turn into the perpetrators who diminish dignity and rights.

9.1 The DynCorp Case

According to experts of the UN Mission in Bosnia and Herzegovina (hereinafter UNMIBH) and nongovernmental organizations (NGOs), trafficking of human beings first began to appear in 1995, just after the soldiers and peacekeepers came into the country (Human Rights Watch, 2002). The sudden influx of trafficked women and girls was no coincidence, as Bosnia and Herzegovina (hereinafter BiH) fitted the bill for a healthy breeding ground. As Bolkovac and Lynn (2011, p. 85), who served for the private military company DynCorp during the UNMBIH, describes, "human trafficking follows a predictable path of infestation: it seeks out environments that are warm with tumult, such as the aftermath of war or the fall of communism. Then it preys on desperate victims who are brought in over porous borders and past bribable guards. Strategically, it breeds near a region teeming with internationals, because they are the ones who have the money to feed it."

The moment international police, civilian contractors, and international peacekeepers entered the country, BiH was a transitional and developing state with weak

© The Author(s) 2018

C. Cole, R. Vermeltfoort, *U.S. Government Contractors and Human Trafficking*, SpringerBriefs in Criminology, https://doi.org/10.1007/978-3-319-70827-0_9

law enforcement and a weak police system. Within this situation, traffickers had little fear for punishment or criminal prosecution for their crimes as trafficking laws went largely unenforced. The Human Rights Watch report (2002) estimated that during the UNMBIH as many as 2000 women and girls, mostly trafficked from Moldova, Romania, and Ukraine, were captured in Bosnian brothels, masquerading as hotels, bars, and cafés throughout the country. The women and girls were falsely imprisoned and deprived of their passports, held in debt bondage, forced to have sex with clients, and beaten when they refused to comply with the demands of the brothel owners. The women who were accepted in the shelters in Sarajevo exhibited psychological trauma and serious physical injuries as cigarette burns, syphilis, (gynecological) infections, fractures, and head injuries (Human Rights Watch, 2002). The International Organization for Migration even reported victims as young as 13 (Human Rights Watch, 2002). Research done by Human Rights Watch and local NGOs indicated that almost 90% of the brothel use since 1995 could be attributed to peacekeeping operations personnel (Human Rights Watch, 2002). The fact that brothels usually emerged close to IPTF bases is suggested as evidence of this practice (Simic, 2004).

The alleged direct involvement of peacekeepers ranges from visiting and/or using the sexual services of trafficked women to actual smuggling. There are allegations of IPTF officers supporting the transport of trafficked women by forging documents and tipping of club owners of planned raids (Murray, 2003; Mendelson, 2005). In addition to the direct and principal perpetrators of human trafficking, there was a vast majority of individuals within the subunit, headquarters of DynCorp, and the US government who facilitated the crimes by knowingly turning a blind eye and endeavoring a cover-up (Human Rights Watch, 2002). In her book *The Whistleblower*, former DynCorp employee Kathryn Bolkovac describes a major cover-up attempt by DynCorp management, both in the subunit and in the headquarters. Bolkovac found out about the misconduct of her colleagues right after she interviewed a Moldavian girl who arrived at the IPTF station where Bolkovac was working. During the interview, she could only understand one word, "Florida," which she knew was a name of nightclub where she had often seen UN vehicles (Bolkovac and Lynn, 2011, p. 77). When Bolkovac arrived at the nightclub, it was abandoned, which allowed her to go inside and check the area. In an open safe, Bolkovac found passports of foreign women and hundreds of US dollars, which were only available at the American military base (Bolkovac and Lynn, 2011). Bolkovac tried to stop the criminal behavior of her colleagues by reporting the misconduct to her employer, DynCorp. Instead of taking her case seriously, Bolkovac describes that case files implicating the involvement of DynCorp personnel in human trafficking suddenly disappeared and some investigations were cancelled. Moreover, rather than rewarding Bolkovac for reporting the misconduct, she was fired. The same happened to a second whistleblower, Johnston, who explains he actually witnessed "co-workers and supervisors literally buying and selling women for their own personal enjoyment" (Human Rights Watch, 2002).

The cooperation of state officials and local police departments from its beginning enabled the sex trafficking scene to flourish. According to Blaustein (2012), it was the combination of outright corruption, state incompetence, and lack of political will that enabled sex traffickers to violate the law with impunity. As DynCorp employees had the responsibility to advise and monitor the local Bosnian police, they were the ones designated to end this impunity. However, instead of rescuing the enslaved girls and investigate the traffickers and corrupt local police, a vast group of DynCorp employees turned a blind eye or even cooperated with the local police and traffickers in the billion dollar sex industry.

9.2 Research Question

How can we explain that the ones designated to protect human rights, in fact, turn into the perpetrators who diminish dignity and rights? This thesis tries to unravel the factors that contributed to the widespread transformation of peacekeepers into perpetrators in post-war Bosnia. Even though some form of complicity in human trafficking was widespread among peacekeepers during the UNMBIH, the involvement of employees of the Private Military and Security Company (hereinafter PMSC) DynCorp was best documented. Therefore, this thesis selected DynCorp and their complicity in the crimes during the UNMBIH as its case study. The main research question of this thesis sounds as follows:

> *How can we explain the widespread transformation process of DynCorp employees from peacekeepers into perpetrators of sex trafficking and endeavoring a cover-up of the scandal during the UNMBIH? And to what extent can this transformation be explained by subunit analysis and a bidirectional approach?*

Even though DynCorp's response to the involvement of their personnel in rape and sex trafficking consisted of shearing of the problem to a few "rotten apples," this thesis argues that the multifaceted nature of the crimes requires a more complex explanation. Even though human trafficking is a crime committed by individuals, this thesis argues that our theoretical understanding of the transformation process of DynCorp employees into perpetrators must extend beyond individual-level explanations. This thesis will analyze the transformation process of DynCorp employees into perpetrators within the context of the social organization, as DynCorp was responsible for the opportunity structure and lack of social control mechanisms that facilitated the acts of human trafficking during the UNMBIH.

In addition, the case study of this thesis shows a complex entanglement and symbiotic relationship between private actors and state actors. Whereas DynCorp deployed the individual perpetrators, the Private Military and Security Company was in turn hired by the United States. As the explanatory power of the committed crimes is scattered over these different layers, including the state, this thesis takes state-corporate crime theory as the starting point in its quest for explanatory factors. State-corporate crime theory, as a new category of crime, uses a top-down approach, whereby institutional factors influence the choices of corporations, which in turn determine the behavior of individuals within the corporation (Kauzlarich and Kramer,

1998a, 1998b). This thesis will analyze to what extent the transformation process of DynCorp employees during the UNMBIH can be explained by top-down mechanisms originating in the institutional level. In addition, in their quest for explanatory factors for corporate criminal behavior, state-corporate crime theory considers the corporation as one level of analysis. The important question is whether viewing DynCorp as one level of analysis fails to notice the possible differences, with regard to environment and manner of involvement in the crimes, between the headquarters in the home state, the United States, and the subunit in the host state, Bosnia. Even though state-corporate crime theory mentions the subunit goals as a motivational factor on the organizational level, this literature does not examine the opportunity structure and operationality of control within the subunit in explaining the crimes. This thesis will analyze to what extent the transformation process of DynCorp employees can be explained when DynCorp is examined as one level of analysis.

After applying state-corporate crime theory and the associated theoretical model on the DynCorp case, this thesis will mention the shortcomings of the original theory and model in explaining the widespread transformation process of DynCorp employees into perpetrators during the UNMBIH. Subsequently, this thesis will present a revised theoretical framework, with the subunit as a separate level of analysis. This addition enables the framework to examine the motivation, opportunity structure, and operationality of control of the subunit within DynCorp during the UNMBIH. It moreover enables the framework to examine the possible complex interplays, both top-down and bottom-up, between the headquarters in the home state and the subunit in the host state in explaining the crimes.

9.3 Methodology

This thesis will be a case study of DynCorp and their complicity in sex trafficking and endeavoring a cover-up of these crimes during the UNMBIH. As defined by George and Bennett (2005, p. 27), a case study is "the detailed examination of an aspect of a historical episode to develop or test historical explanations that may be generalizable to other events." Even though some form of complicity in sex trafficking was widespread among peacekeepers during the UNMBIH, the involvement of DynCorp employees was best documented and proven, which certifies its selection as the subject of study in this thesis.

This thesis uses case study as its research method, as it enables this thesis to look at a large number of intervening variables and examine the operation of complex causal mechanisms in the widespread transformation process of peacekeepers into perpetrators. Moreover, a detailed consideration of contextual factors obtained from extensive NGO reports and interviews with an expert and a participant who were present in Bosnia during the UNMBIH provides the potential for achieving high conceptual validity. These strengths of a case method make it particularly useful for theory development in this thesis. The case study of DynCorp and their complicity in crimes will be examined with a deviant theoretical approach. There are no theories in the literature that examine the power of subunits with both a top-down and bottom-up approach within the bigger macro, meso, and micro context. Through the analysis of the case study with both a top-down and bottom-up approach, this thesis aims to develop a new theory by inductively identifying new variables or causal mechanisms. The intensive study of a case that fails to fit existing theories may provide significant theoretical insights (George and Bennett, 2005). This may lead to new generalizations when it uncovers new causal mechanisms that prove to be applicable to a wide range of cases.

In addition, this thesis will use the method of process tracing to generate new hypotheses and variables on the basis of events observed inductively in the case study. The method of process tracing is an attempt to trace the links between possible causes and observed outcomes within a particular historical case (George & Bennett, 2005). Through process tracing this thesis tries to convert a historical narrative into an analytical causal explanation couched in explicit theoretical forms. According to George and Bennett (2005), some historians criticize this procedure of transforming a detailed and rich historical explanation into selective and abstract theoretical concepts. They argue that unique characteristics of the explanation inevitably will be lost in the process. This thesis agrees that information will be lost in any effort at theory formulation. However, in line with George and Bennett (2005), this thesis argues that this loss does not necessarily jeopardize the validity of the conclusions obtained from the case for the theory and its utility.

For the method of process, tracing this thesis uses literature study and in-depth interviews as its research methods. With regard to the literature study, this thesis will approach and analyze academic literature from a criminological perspective. This multidisciplinary perspective provides theoretical insights from a variety of disciplines, including political science, history, sociology, (international) law, and psychology. The specific subject of this thesis makes it virtually impossible to solely rely on academic sources. Lack of access to the practices of DynCorp during the UNMBIH necessitates the use of media articles, NGO reports, and research of supranational organizations. Even though these sources provide a lot of information, the reliability of these sources, which are (often) not produced for academic purposes, cannot be granted. This thesis will parallel and combine as many different nonacademic sources as possible to overcome this methodological disadvantage. Moreover, there may be possible biases and partisanship when interpreting the sources. The researcher is aware of this methodological disadvantage and will remain as objective as possible at every stage of the process, by constantly taking distance from the described arguments and consider possible counterarguments. In addition to a literature study and meta-analysis, the researcher also conducted two in-depth interviews with a participant and area expert who were present in Bosnia during the UNMBIH for on-the-ground information and to substantiate the transformation of descriptive explanations into analytical explanations. Even though the best explanations for the transformation process of DynCorp employees may be obtained by researching the perceptions from a perpetrators' perspective, this is almost impossible due to the sensitivity and accessibility of the subject. However, in the absence of a perpetrators' perspective, the researcher obtained an understanding of the transformation process by interviewing a participant who was situated in the same environment and organizational context and therefore subject to the same explanatory factors as the perpetrators. This semi-structured interview was conducted with Kathryn Bolkovac, a former DynCorp employee who decided to blow the whistle on the misconduct of her colleagues during the UNMBIH. In addition, as the explanatory power of the transformation process is scattered over different macro, meso, and micro layers, the researcher also aimed at interviewing an individual from a higher rank. The second semi-structured interview was therefore conducted with Madeleine Rees, who was the Head of the UN Office of the High Commissionaire for Human Rights in BiH during the mission. As noted by George and Bennett (2005), studying a case with archival research and interviews with participants and area experts has powerful advantages in the identification of new variables. In this thesis, these new variables will be implemented in the existing state-corporate crime theory.

9.4 Structure

This thesis consists of seven chapters. Chapter 9 is the current introduction, while Chap. 10 will investigate the origin and challenges of the privatization of the military in general in order to understand the complex entanglement and symbiotic relationship between private actors and state actors in the DynCorp case. Chapter 11 sets out the contextual framework of the main criminal activities in the DynCorp case. This chapter examines to what extent the committed crimes of human trafficking and endeavoring a cover-up can be regarded as international crimes. In addition, it substantiates why this thesis examines the individual criminal behavior of human trafficking during the UNMBIH as organizational crime. The manner in which this functional interdependency between corporations and states can lead to injurious or illegal social action is described by state-corporate crime theory, which will be described in Chap. 12. This chapter explicates the concept of state-corporate crime and explains why this theory will be used for the purpose of this thesis. This chapter moreover presents and describes the original integrated theoretical framework on state-corporate crime. Chapter 13 will analyze the actual case study of this thesis, DynCorp, and their complicity in international crimes. This chapter has an explanatory character and tries to explain the widespread transformation process of DynCorp employees into perpetrators by applying the original theoretical framework on state-corporate crime to the case. After the close examination of the case study, Chap. 14 will describe the shortcomings of the original theory and model on state-corporate crime in explaining the transformation process of DynCorp employees during the UNMBIH. This chapter substantiates the power of subunit analysis when explaining these crimes and presents a revised theoretical framework. The revised framework enables the examination of subunits and their complex interrelationships with the other levels of analysis to explain the crimes committed by PMSCs. Chapter 15 finally consists of a discussion of the research and its effects on existing theories and provides recommendations for further research.

Chapter 10
Private Military and Security Companies

A unique characteristic of the organizational crime committed by DynCorp, and often by PMSCs in general, is that it shows functional interdependency between corporations and governments. In order to answer the main research question of this thesis and understand these contemporary complex relationships between the public and the private sector that can lead to illegal or injurious social action, we have to investigate the origin of the privatized military and the challenges it brought into the world of military and beyond. Therefore, this chapter will describe the developments toward and the characteristics and challenges of the privatization of military and security tasks. In the first section, the focus will be on the coinciding developments that facilitated the formation of the private military and security industry. In the following paragraph, the typical characteristics of PMSCs and the market for force will be discussed. The final paragraph of this chapter discusses the challenges of working with PMSCs.

10.1 Developments Toward the Privatization of Military and Security Tasks

In 1993, the shocking images of Somali rebels dragging the lifeless body of an American soldier through the streets of Mogadishu changed the world of military (Singer, 2001). The images of the disastrous peacekeeping mission in Somalia, in combination with the end of the Cold War, caused reluctance among industrialized economies to send in their own troops for peacekeeping missions. This deficit of national armies in the military sector was increasingly replaced by PMSCs: "legally established enterprises that make a profit, by either providing services involving the potential exercise of armed force in a systematic way and by military means, and/or by the transfer of that potential to clients through training and other practices, such as logistics support, equipment procurement, and intelligence gathering" (Ortiz,

© The Author(s) 2018

C. Cole, R. Vermeltfoort, *U.S. Government Contractors and Human Trafficking*, SpringerBriefs in Criminology, https://doi.org/10.1007/978-3-319-70827-0_10

2004, p. 206). PMSCs, who gradually gained more responsibility during peacekeeping operations, changed the world of modern warfare. Between 1990 and 2001, the number of PMSCs increased from 50 military officers for every one contractor to a ratio of ten soldiers to every one private contractor (Singer, 2001). In addition, the total number of PMSCs hired by the UN in 2013 was 43, and the total number of personnel serving in peacekeeping operations was 111, 113 (WILPF, 2013).

Three coinciding developments caused the worldwide expansion of the private military industry in the early 1990s (Singer, 2001). First, the changes in supply and demand of armed forces after the Cold War created a gap in the security market. The end of the Cold War increased cooperation between the permanent members of the Security Council and created positive expectations about the role of the UN in maintaining peace and security in the world. Due to this positive outlook, the number of international peacekeeping missions increased noticeably, which provided opportunities for the emerging industry of PMSCs. Secondly, transformation of warfare and technological developments on weaponry enabled small groups to obtain large, destructive weapons. The advancing technology ensured that private actors in the area of operation itself could execute the information and communication technology (ICT) and maintenance of previously complex weapons. In some cases, military systems critical to combat, such as unmanned aircrafts, were even put in the hands of citizens. The third development that caused the worldwide expansion of the private military and security industry was the so-called power of privatization and privatization of power. The term privatization is often associated with positive effects as increased quality, efficiency, and low costs. The positive effects of privatization in other areas gave the push and legitimacy to privatize more tasks that were previously carried out by governments. According to Singer (2001), it was no surprise that the phenomenon of privatization was gradually applied to the military realm as well.

10.2 The Market for Force

The continued growth of the private military industry results in a gradual breakdown of the monopoly over violence by the state (Singer, 2001). According to the AIV (2007), the use of PMSCs for the logistics of the combat units is more attractive and efficient, especially in times of "peace." This argument is substantiated by the fact that PMSCs only need to be paid when they are needed, while national armies are continuously paid, even when they are in their barracks. Another expected positive effect of the privatization of military and security tasks, according to Singer (2011), is that their relative discipline and market incentives to good behavior may limit them from engaging in illegal behavior as their long-term profit line depends on their public image. However, Singer (2011, p. 228) describes that the issue is not that simple. "Just as in the rest of commerce, war is business where nice firms do not always finish first. Aspirations of corporate responsibility and a positive public image may be overridden by the need to fulfill a contract or be seen as an effective firm that gets things done." Historians often remark that in this unregulated world of private actors, anything could be bought for a price, which results in extortion, corruption, and crime (Sklansky, 1998).

The clientele of PMSCs is not limited to states but ranges across the moral spectrum: from humanitarian organizations and multinational corporations to warlords and dictators. However, research by the International Peace Operations Association (IPOA, 2006) shows that national governments (62%) are the dominant users of PMSCs. The remaining percentage of customers includes the private sector (29%), individuals (6%), and nongovernmental organizations (3%). As national governments are the dominant users of PMSCs, these private corporations could not have developed or functioned without the economic, legal, and political infrastructure as provided by the government (Sklar, 1988). In turn, governments depend on corporations to provide the economic base in the form of corporate profits and individual salaries and to supply necessary services and goods (Offe & Ronge, 1982). In fact, the privatization of the military resulted in "bilateral dependency" in which states, as buyers, and PMSCs as sellers of services became mutually interdependent (Baum & McGahan, 2009).

10.3 Challenges of Private Military Companies

One of the biggest differences between a PMSC and a national army is the fact that PMSCs are profit-driven actors who are primarily responsible to their shareholders. The primary goal of military personnel, as national servants of their country, is to end wars. On the other hand, private corporations are mainly focused on financial interests. As noted by Baum and McGahan (2009, p. 2), "PMSCs profit from conflict, and thus may not pursue peace even when resolution does not compromise the interests of the contracting sovereign." This commercial aspect that characterizes PMSCs creates a continuous tension between the interests of the local population and the interests of the PMSC. This tension may result in a situation wherein the PMSC misuses its power by prioritizing its own interests above the interests of the local population.

In addition, the privatization of the military brings forth multiple challenges when it comes to law enforcement, transparency, and accountability. As neither mercenaries nor soldiers, PMSCs do not fit easily into consisting forms of action and legislation of the host country, the country of origin, or international law (Cutler, 2010). Due to the fact that the host country is often a transitional and weak state, those governments often lack the effective control necessary to target private actors. With regard to the states of origins, Ryngaert (2008) notes that states are reluctant to exercise extraterritorial jurisdiction to target their private actors, as they are reserved in violating the sovereignty of the host state. Yet, in 2000, the United States adopted the Military Extraterritorial Jurisdiction Act (hereinafter MEJA) as a response to misconduct by PMSCs in the 1990s. Even though the MEJA enables the United States to target American private contractors under the American legal system, it also shows major limitations. In fact, the MEJA can only be applied to US citizens that committed an offense that would, under the American legal system, lead to an imprisonment of 1 year (AIV, 2007).

A reason for the absence of applicable law to target private actors may be the lack of transparency around the tasks and scope of PMSCs. By hiring PMSCs governments can increase the flexibility of deployment and escape political constraints as maximum military capacities. According to Singer (2001, 2007), as compared to the use of national armies, the use of PMSCs obscures political responsibility and legal liability and complicates democratic control. Another factor that decreases transparency is the fact that casualties involving PMSCs are often left out of official statistics and are less reported in the media. As Singer (2007, p. 5) notes, "while private forces make up about 50% of the overall operation on Iraq, they have been mentioned in only a quarter of one percent of all American media stories." In addition to lack of transparency, there is lack of accountability surrounding the use of PMSCs. Despite a century-long debate, the question who should make the decisions when working with private actors and why remains unanswered. However, the fact that PMSCs are often the primary source of authority during peacekeeping missions emphasizes the importance of their accountability (Picarelli, 2002). As Cameron (2006, p. 577) notes, "the private military company industry is clearly multifaceted and complex, operating around the globe in many different situations."

Chapter 11
Sex Trafficking and Endeavoring a Cover-Up as International Crimes

This chapter will describe and legally and criminologically classify the main criminal activities in the DynCorp-case. The committed crimes by DynCorp during the UNMBIH, as the "what" in this thesis, include sex trafficking and knowingly endeavoring a cover-up for the first crime. The first section legally defines the crime of sex trafficking and examines to what extent these criminal activities during the UNMBIH can in legal terms be viewed as an international crime. The second section of this thesis focuses on the second crime during the UNMBIH, namely, knowingly endeavoring a cover-up for the first crime. This section examines to what extent the cover-up in the DynCorp-case can be viewed as a (international) crime. In addition, even though both crimes are committed by individuals, the third paragraph of this chapter substantiates why this thesis examines this individual criminal behavior during the UNMBIH as organizational crime.

11.1 Sex Trafficking as an International Crime

In order to examine whether the crime of sex trafficking could be classified as an international crime, we first need to determine that the practices during the UNMBIH indeed constitute crimes of human trafficking. Human trafficking under the Trafficking Protocol requires that trafficking is being carried out with deception or coercion and for the purpose of exploitation (Obokata, 2005). The implicated involvement of DynCorp personnel ranged from using the services of women in brothels to actually buying passports from traffickers and brothel owners to keep the women and girls at their own residence (Simic, 2004; Bolkovac and Lynn, 2011). With the more severe forms of involvement, we could argue that buying and withholding passports for the purpose of holding women and girls in your own residence indeed constitutes a crime of human trafficking. Furthermore, as sex trafficking was a main focus area for DynCorp employees, one may argue that the DynCorp

© The Author(s) 2018

C. Cole, R. Vermeltfoort, *U.S. Government Contractors and Human Trafficking*,
SpringerBriefs in Criminology, https://doi.org/10.1007/978-3-319-70827-0_11

employees that visited the brothels should have known that the brothels that suddenly arose around their base camps contained trafficking victims (Human Rights Watch, 2002). If the DynCorp employees indeed knew about the trafficking scheme, visiting these brothels could make them complicit in the crime of human trafficking.

Now that we have legally defined the crime of human trafficking, we can examine to what extent we can legally classify these acts of sex trafficking as international crimes. The Rome Statute distinguishes three international crimes for which individuals can be held accountable, namely, genocide, crimes against humanity, and (both non-international and international) war crimes. War crimes are violations of the laws of war committed in times of armed conflict, which are described in the Geneva Conventions of 1949. As the direct and indirect involvement of DynCorp in sex trafficking occurred in times of peace, these crimes cannot be labeled as war crimes. In addition, as the acts of sex trafficking in the DynCorp-case have not been committed with the intent to destroy, in whole or in part, a national, ethical, racial, or religious group, they cannot be classified as genocide. However, when part of a widespread and systematic practice, sex trafficking can be seen as a crime against humanity. Case law supports the claim that sex trafficking could qualify as a crime against humanity. One example is the Kunarac case, in which the Trial Chamber of the International Criminal Tribunal for the former Yugoslavia (ICTY) held that human trafficking could be qualified as a crime against humanity, namely, the crime of enslavement (Obokata, 2005). Furthermore, the crime of enslavement is listed under Article 7 of the Rome Statute of the International Criminal Court (ICC). Article 7 (2) provides the following definition of the crime of enslavement:

> *Enslavement means the exercise of any or all of the powers attaching to the right of ownership over a person and includes the exercise of such power in the course of trafficking in persons, in particular women and children.*

Before the crimes of sex trafficking during the UNMBIH can be qualified as international crimes, certain elements must be established. First, the crimes need to have a widespread and systematic character. Widespread in this regard implies that the nature in the crimes is large scale and it involves a multiplicity of victims, and systematic refers to the organized nature of the crimes. Secondly, there must be intent to commit the underlying offence, which also may be for personal reasons (Smeulers & Grünfeld, 2011; Mendelson, 2005).

Even though a total number of sex trafficking victims do not exist, the available facts suggest that the nature of the crimes was large scale and involved a multiplicity of victims. First, in the mid-1990s the number of women trafficked into BiH drastically increased, which indicates the widespread character of trafficking (Mendelson, 2005). The Human Rights Watch (2002) supports this claim by stating that investigations "uncovered conclusive evidence of widespread trafficking of women and girls into the sex industry throughout both Bosnian entities, the Federation of Bosnia and Herzegovina and Republika Srpska" (Human Rights Watch, 2002). The systematic character of the crimes is reflected in the strong connections between the government and the Serbian mafia (Corpwatch, 2002). Furthermore, the crimes of sex trafficking were not simply individual actions but involved a chain of command, as the crimes were occurring with the knowledge of high-ranking officials, and they did not intervene to stop it.

11.2 Endeavoring a Cover-Up as an International Crime

The previous section examined whether the practices of sex trafficking during the UNMBIH constitute crimes of human trafficking and whether these acts could be legally classified as international crimes. In addition to the principal and complicit perpetrators of sex trafficking, there was a vast majority of individuals within the subunit, headquarters of DynCorp, and the US government who facilitated the crimes by knowingly turning a blind eye and endeavoring a cover-up (Human Rights Watch, 2002). Even though endeavoring a cover-up does not directly constitute criminal behavior, one could argue that knowingly covering up the issue made DynCorp complicit to the commitment of the crimes. As stated in Article 30 of the Rome Statute, a person shall be criminally responsible and liable for punishment for a crime if the material elements are committed with intent and knowledge. Even though the Rome Statute solely focuses on criminal liability of individuals, it is possible to argue that this intent and knowledge criteria could also be applied to corporations. As high-ranking officials are closely related to the corporation, one could argue that in the case of shared knowledge and intent of the circumstances among a vast majority of high-ranking officials, one could speak of knowledge and intent of the corporation. This mental element of knowledge of a crime is often referred to as dolus eventualis or conditional intent. In the DynCorp-case, the awareness of high-ranking officials, and therefore of the corporation, of the complicity of DynCorp personnel in sex trafficking in BiH was emphasized when former DynCorp officer Kathryn Bolkovac contested her dismissal in court (Employment Tribunals, 2002).

In October 2000, former DynCorp employee Kathryn Bolkovac sent an email to about 50 mission personnel, including high-ranking officials within DynCorp and the UN, about her discovery of the involvement of multiple DynCorp colleagues in a huge human trafficking scene. The email with the title "do not read this if you have a weak stomach or guilty conscience" revealed all details of the human trafficking scene and the involvement of DynCorp personnel in it (Information Memorandum to the State Department, 2000). Instead of taking disciplinary actions against the perpetrators, DynCorp decided to fire Kathryn Bolkovac for not correctly filling in her time sheets. A trial in court confirmed that Bolkovacs' dismissal was unjustified. The emails and memos from Bolkovac that were used as evidence during her court case prove that a vast majority of high-ranking officials, and therefore the corporation, were aware of the circumstances in BiH (Information Memorandum to the State Department 2000) and may therefore fulfill the knowledge criteria as stated in Article 30 of the Rome Statute.

In addition to knowledge, Article 30 of the Rome Statute mentions intent with regard to the material element as a criterion for criminal liability. According to the Rome Statute, a person has intent with regard to a consequence when that person means to cause that consequence or is aware that it will occur in the ordinary course of events. One could argue that DynCorp knew that their decision to endeavor a cover-up instead of taking disciplinary actions would facilitate the widespread and systematic acts of sex trafficking.

11.3 Rotten Apples or a Rotten Barrel

The previous two sections examined whether the practices during the UNMBIH constitute crimes of human trafficking and whether these acts and endeavoring a cover-up of these acts could legally be classified as international crimes. This section examines whether the human trafficking and endeavoring a cover-up during UNMBIH can be regarded as organizational crimes or whether they were committed for the benefit of individual criminals without support of the organization, which would classify them as occupational crimes (Sutherland, 1940). With regard to the cover-up by DynCorp, one could argue that it was a clear example of organizational crime as it was committed with organizational support that is furthering its own ends. DynCorp may have supported the decision to cover up the complicity of their employees in sex trafficking because of damage control and the fundamental desire to protect its own image and legitimacy. In addition, endeavoring a cover-up may have prevented the loss of the million-dollar contract. Even though one may conceptualize the cover-up as an example of organizational crime, this is more difficult with regard to the act of sex trafficking during the UNMBIH. One could argue that the direct and indirect involvement of isolated DynCorp employees in trafficking cases, which were participatory for their own benefit and without support of the corporation, could be viewed as occupational crime. In line with this reasoning, DynCorp's response to the involvement of their personnel in rape and trafficking consisted of shearing of the problem to a few "rotten apples." However, the current paragraph substantiates why the "rotten apple" approach cannot fully explain the involvement of DynCorp employees in sex trafficking and rape during the UNMBIH.

The numerous cases of the involvement of peacekeepers in sex trafficking and rape (Haiti, Sudan, Kosovo, and the Democratic Republic of the Congo) during the past decades suggest that the explanation of the crimes goes beyond just rotten apple explanations. In addition, the rotten apple theory could not explain why the involvement of peacekeepers in sex trafficking was so widespread and organized during the UNMBIH. The perspective of this thesis parallels the findings of White and Terry (2008), who revised the rotten apple explanation through a close examination of police deviance and sexual abuse in the Catholic Church. White and Terry (2008, p. 659) argue, "like police brutality, the full explanation for child sexual abuse among Catholic clergy does not rest solely with deviant sexual interests of a few rotten apples. Instead, the profession itself plays a contributing role much more in the same way that the working environment of the police plays a role in police brutality." The DynCorp-case shows similarities with cleric abuse and police deviance, as they can be regarded as bureaucratic institutions that share organizational elements that facilitate deviance. As noted by White and Terry (2008), these features include a division of labor and the existence of a distinct subunit that is governed by informal rules that value maintaining the status quo, secrecy, and autonomy and is defined by solidarity and social isolation. Chapters 11 and 12 of this thesis will show that these features were also present in the DynCorp-case.

In line with the reasoning of White and Terry (2008), this thesis argues that our theoretical understanding of involvement of peacekeepers in sex trafficking must extend beyond individual-level explanations. This thesis adopts the same argument as White and Terry (2008) for police officers and priests that DynCorp employees did not join the UNMBIH with the expressed goal of getting involved in sex trafficking. Even though DynCorp tried to portray the scandal as an act of isolated rotten apples, an examination shows that there also was a level of organizational responsibility. Firstly, DynCorp recruited people who were about to or had actually been fired for charges as sexual harassment against women (interview Bolkovac, 2014). In addition, the organization provided the opportunity structures and lack of social control mechanisms that facilitated (the complicity in acts of) sex trafficking. In this regard, we could state that DynCorp allowed for the occurrence of sex trafficking during the UNMBIH. Therefore, this thesis will examine the crimes as organizational crime and analyze the transformation process of DynCorp employees into perpetrators within the context of the social organization.

Chapter 12
Theoretical Framework

Chapter 10 described the complex relationship and mutual interdependency between private and public actors, with regard to military and security tasks in peacekeeping missions, as the congruent effect of the privatization of these tasks. The manner in which this functional interdependency between corporations and governments can lead to illegal or injurious social action is described by state-corporate crime theory. The current chapter will analyze to what extent the DynCorp-case can be viewed as an example of state-corporate crime. In order to do so, the criminological concept of state-corporate crime will be explained. Therefore, the first section of this chapter will explicate the concept of "state-corporate crime" and explain why this theory will be used for the purpose of this thesis. To analyze state-corporate crimes, Kramer and Michalowski (1990) created and Kauzlarich and Kramer (1998a) revised an integrated theoretical framework. The second section will present Kauzlarich and Kramer's integrated theoretical model and describe their argumentation for the classification of the schedule in three levels of analysis and three catalysts for action. In Chap. 13, this analytical framework will be used as a starting point in explaining why DynCorp employees turned into perpetrators during the UNMBIH.

12.1 State-Corporate Crime

The concept of state-corporate crime was introduced by Kramer in 1990 to specify a specific type of organizational crime. State-corporate crime finds its origin in two distinct forms of white-collar crime, namely, corporate crime and state crime. Corporate crime involves "any act committed by corporations that is punished by the state, regardless of whether it is punished under administrative, civil or criminal law" (Clinard & Yeager, 1980, p. 16). State crime and state-organized crime are "acts defined by law as criminal and committed by state officials in the pursuit of their jobs as representatives of the state" (Chambliss, 1989, p. 183). The central

© The Author(s) 2018

C. Cole, R. Vermeltfoort, *U.S. Government Contractors and Human Trafficking*, SpringerBriefs in Criminology, https://doi.org/10.1007/978-3-319-70827-0_12

focus of both corporate and state-crime theory lays on the complex relationships between state actors and private actors, in particular corporations. The assemblage of corporate crime and state-crime theory formed the origin of state-corporate crime theory. Kramer (1990a) defined state-corporate crime as follows (p. 1):

> *State-corporate crime is defined as an illegal or socially injurious social action that is the collective product of the interaction between a business corporation and a state agency in a joint endeavor. These crimes involve the active participation of two or more organizations, at least one of which is private and one of which is public. They are the harmful result of an inter-organizational relationship between business and government.*

Kramer and Michalowski (1993) argued that the inter-organizational relationship as mentioned in this definition could take two distinct forms, namely, state-facilitated and state-initiated state-corporate crime. State-facilitated state-corporate crimes occur "when government regulatory institutions fail to restrain deviant business activities, either because of direct collusion between the two or because they adhere to shared goals whose attainment would be hampered by aggressive regulation." State-initiated state-corporate crime, on the other hand, occurs "when corporations, employed by the government, engage in organizational deviance at the direction of, or with the tacit approval of, the government" (Kramer, Michalowski, & Kauzlarich, 2002, p. 271).

To what extent can the theory of state-corporate crime be applied to the DynCorp-case as the subject of this thesis? In order to answer this question, one has to investigate whether there is an "inter-organizational relationship" between a business corporation and a state agency. It is clear that the US government is a state agency and that DynCorp is a business corporation as it is driven by the same business motivators as other commercial entities, such as corporate sustainability, growth, shareholder value, profit, and achievement. The inter-organizational relationship between business and government is reflected in the direct link between DynCorp as the seller and the US government as the buyer of logistical and technology services. After the Bosnian war, the Dayton Peace Agreement created the IPTF consisting of international police, civilian contractors, and international peacekeepers from nearly 50 UN member states. The UN member states often selected officers from their national police forces to staff the IPTF in BiH. However, in the absence of a national police force, the United States of America contracted and therefore depended on DynCorp for the recruitment of monitors from local and state police departments. As the DynCorp-case shows an inter-organizational relationship between a business corporation and state agency, the concept and theory of state-corporate crime can and will be applied to the case study of this thesis.

12.2 The Integrated Model of Kauzlarich and Kramer

The previous section demonstrated that the DynCorp-case could be viewed as an example of state-corporate crime. In addition to introducing the concept of state-corporate crime, Kramer and Michalowski (1990) presented an integrated theoretical framework that can be used to analyze state-corporate crimes. This thesis will use the integrated model as a starting point to explain the widespread transformation process of DynCorp employees into perpetrators during the UNMBIH. The theoretical framework, which was revised by Kauzlarich and Kramer (1998a), incorporated the three major theoretical approaches to the study of corporate crime at that time, namely, differential association theory, organizational theory, and the theory of political economy. The central focus of their theoretical model is on the complex interplays and interdependence of corporations and governments. The central thought of their theory is that horizontal and vertical relationships between corporations and governments comprehend powerful potentials for the creation of social harm. The integrated theoretical model therefore enables this thesis to examine the case study with a multidimensional approach, where organizational and institutional forces conjoin with definitional and cultural processes in the production of conditions favorable to organizational crime. It moreover enables this thesis to analyze the crimes committed by DynCorp through the examination of the functional interdependency and complex interplays between DynCorp and the US government.

The integrated theoretical model of state-corporate crime (Table 12.1) explicates different factors that may contribute to the production of social harm on three levels of analysis: the institutional (1), organizational (2), and individual level (3). Furthermore, the model divides the factors on these different levels of analysis into three catalysts for action, namely, motivation (1), opportunity structure (2), and operationality of control (3). The integrated theoretical model indicates the key factors that may contribute to or restrain corporate deviance at each intersection of a catalyst for action and a level of analysis.

The three levels of analysis in the integrated theoretical model of state-corporate crime are supported by different criminological theories. The interaction level of analysis focuses on individuals and explicates the factors derived from social-psychological theories in explaining organizational crime. This approach formed the main perspective of the first white-collar crime theorists. A prime example of one of the first theories to be applied to white-collar crime with a micro approach was Sutherland's differential association theory (Sutherland, 1949, 1956). This theory argues that criminal behavior is formed when individuals interact within personal, intimate groups and are isolated from those who regard such behavior unfavorably. According to the differential association theory, a person may engage in criminal behavior when the weight of the unfavorable definitions falls short of the favorable definitions. In the early years of white-collar crime research, the differential association theory found partial support by a number of criminologists (Albanese, 1982b; Clinard, 1946; Cressey, 1950; Lane, 1953). In addition, a more recent theory by Hirschi and Gottfredson (1987, 1989) also examined white-collar crime with a micro approach. This theory argues that the essence of criminal behavior lies in low self-control of individuals and their pursuit of self-interest. Weak ties to the community and faulty socialization cause low self-control, which may result in the use of fraud and force to achieve immediate gratification (Gottfredson & Hirschi, 1990).

Table 12.1 An integrated theoretical model of state-corporate crime

		Catalysts for action	
Level of analysis	Motivation	Opportunity structure	Operationality of control
Institutional environment (history, political economy, culture)	Culture of competition Economic pressure Organizational goals Performance emphasis	Availability of legal means Obstacles and constraints Blocked goals/strain Availability of illegal means Access to resources	International reactions Political pressure Legal sanctions Media scrutiny Public opinion Social movements
Organizational (structure and process)	Corporate culture Operative goals Subunit goals Managerial pressure	Instrumental rationality Internal constraints Defective SOPs Creation of illegal means Role specialization Task segregation Computer, telecommunication, And networking technologies Normalization of deviance	Culture of compliance Subculture of resistance Codes of conduct Reward structure Safety and quality control procedures Communication processes
Interaction (face-to-face interaction, individual action)	Socialization Social meaning Individual goals Competitive individualism Material success emphasis	Definitions of situation Perceptions of availability and attractiveness of illegal means	Personal morality Rationalization and techniques of neutralization Separation from consequences Obedience to authority Group think Diffusion of responsibility

Source: From *Crimes of the American Nuclear State: At Home and Abroad,* by David Kauzlarich and Ronald C. Kramer. Copyright 1998 by David Kauzlarich and Ronald C. Kramer. Reprinted with the permission of Northeastern University Press
Note: *SOPs* standard operating procedures

According to Kauzlarich and Kramer (1998a), theories at the micro level can provide important insights in explaining state-corporate crimes. However, they emphasize the lack of incorporation of the organizational and structural level as a major weakness of the micro-level theories. They argue that social-psychological theories fall short in explaining why organizations, as social actors, commit crimes. As noted by Kramer and Michalowski (2006), organizational crime is best understood with a multidimensional empirical analysis with a focus on the interaction effects of political, historical, and contextual factors. Rothe and Mullins (2011) support this observation and criticize traditional criminological inquiry for addressing only one specific level of analysis. The criminologist argues that these theories, by solely explaining the individual-level processes of organizations, external precipitating conditions, or controls, are bound to overlook the complexity of these cases. As noted by Rothe and Mullins (2011, p. 99), "an analysis of complex phenomena shaped by multiple factors such as time-space, history, culture, politics, ideology, and economics must include an integrated model that addresses all levels of analysis: from the structural elements to the individual(s) involved in the crimes." In line with this reasoning, Kauzlarich and Kramer (1998b) inserted the organization and the institutional environment as levels of analysis in their integrated theoretical model of state-corporate crime.

The examination of the organization as a level of analysis found support by organizational theorists arguing that the organization itself instead of their individual employees should be central to the analysis of organizational crime (Albanese, 1982b; Clinard & Yeager, 1980; Ermann & Lundman, 1978; Finney & Lesieur, 1982; Gross, 1978; Schrager & Short, 1978; Vaughan, 1982, 1983). Braithwaite (1985, p. 3) even argued that "theoretical progress began only in the late 1970s when the individualistic theory spawned by the Sutherland tradition was rejected in favor of applying organizational theory paradigms to the phenomenon." The perspective of organizational theorists forms an extension of Merton's traditional criminological theory of anomie (Passas, 1990). These theorists argue that organizations are mainly concerned with performance and achieving goals, while the means to achieve these goals are monitored by weak or absent standards. In addition, when legitimate means to achieve organizational goals are blocked, this may result in such severe strain that organizations resort to illegal solutions (Finney & Lesieur, 1982). Organizational theorists mention two other factors, in addition to performance pressure and strain that may contribute to organizational crime. The first factor is the availability of illegal means. According to Braithwaite (1989), the availability of illegal means for organizational actors to achieve organizational goals increases the likeliness of organizational crime. The second factor, playing an important role in the furtherance of organizational crime, is the environment of social control. According to Finney and Lesieur (1982), when operating problems and a strong performance orientation exist, the occurrence of crime depends on the operationality of social control.

The institutional environment, as the macro level of analysis in the integrated theoretical model of state-corporate crime, deals with the major social institutions of society and the larger social structure. This level of analysis explicates the factors that are derived from theories of political economy. Many scholars emphasize the importance of the interrelationships between political and economic institutions when explaining organizational crime (Barnett, 1981; Box, 1983; Chambliss, 1988, 1989; Messerschmidt, 1986; Michalowski, 1985; Young, 1981). The main assumption of these scholars is that the major impetus for organizational crime stems from corporate capitalism. Capitalism, as an economic system, creates a structure wherein organizations may adhere to illegal means in order to achieve profit. This perspective forms an extension of Merton's strain model, by considering the mode of material production as the accelerant for illegal activity. According to Barnett (1981, p. 5) corporate crime occurs "when management chooses to pursue corporate goals through circumvention of market constraints in a manner prohibited by the state." These crimes may also be committed by the state when it endeavors the creation of optimum conditions for the worldwide operation of its transnational corporations (Kauzlarich & Kramer, 1998b). These crimes committed by a corporation or a state are usually referred to as white-collar crime. Kauzlarich and Kramer (1998b) note that the political economy perspective and the organizational perspective have many similarities. On both levels, the organization is the main focus of analysis, and the emphasis lies on organizational goals and the problems organizations may encounter in achieving these goals by legitimate means. Moreover, both analyze the effect of strain on turning to illegal means and of social control mechanisms in controlling organizational crime.

The integrated theoretical model of state-corporate crime is based on the assertion that criminal behavior within organizations is the result of a coincidence of pressure for goal attainment, available and attractive illegitimate means, and lack of social control mechanisms. Therefore, the model divides the factors on the different levels of analysis into three catalysts for action, namely, motivation, opportunity structure, and operationality of control. In explaining criminal behavior, these three concepts are interdependent. Most criminal behavior involves both motivation and opportunity. As stated by Kauzlarich and Kramer (1998b), "all the motivation in the world to act in a particular way means little if the opportunity to carry out that action is not available." The second catalyst for action in the framework directs attention to the differential distribution of both legal and illegal means to achieve organizational goals. The focus on the distribution of legal and illegal means derives from the proposition in organizational crime literature that when legal means to accomplish goals are blocked, organizational actors will turn to illegal means when they are available. These means, especially when they are illegal, are particularly likely to be selected in the absence of strong social controls, the third core concept in the model. According to the model, the operationality of control mechanism exists at all three levels of analysis. With a top-down approach, the mechanism starts at the institutional level and puts pressure on organizations and its actors. This pressure could consist of various forms of legal sanctions imposed by criminal justice mechanisms or other governmental regulatory bodies on both the domestic and international level. In addition, offending organizations may experience pressure from the domestic or international opinion as expressed in the mass media, citizen watchdog groups, or social movement organizations. At the individual level, strong ethical standards may form a social control mechanism preventing actors to get involved in organizational crime. Therefore, the integrated theoretical model of state-corporate crime emphasizes the importance of examining the effectiveness of existing forces of social control and the ability of organizations to evade or neutralize these control mechanisms.

Chapter 13
Analysis and Explanations

The former chapters examined whether the practices during the UNMBIH substantiated why the committed crimes during the UNMBIH can be seen as organizational crimes and described the complex entanglements and functional interdependency between private and state actors in the DynCorp-case. These findings resulted in the decision to analyze the DynCorp-case with state-corporate crime theory. The current chapter will attempt to take a more explanatory view in answering the "why question." The central research question of this chapter is "how can we explain the widespread transformation process of DynCorp employees from peacekeepers into perpetrators of sex trafficking and endeavoring a cover-up of the scandal during the UNMBIH?" Before examining this research question, it is important to note that within DynCorp, during the UNMBIH, there were different levels and manners of involvement in the crimes. As substantiated in Chap. 1 of this thesis, the personnel in the subunit that trafficked women and girls or cooperated with the traffickers and local police in the furtherance of human trafficking can be viewed as principal perpetrators of these crimes. The employees in the subunit, who knowingly decided to turn a blind eye or cover the issue up, on the other hand, can be regarded as the ones who facilitated the commitment of international crimes. This is also the case for the US government and the corporation in the home state that operated from a distance and facilitated the crimes by endeavoring a cover-up and diminishing the scheme by stating that the misbehavior could be attributed to a couple of bad apples in isolated cases.

In order to answer the research question, as stated above, the integrated theoretical model of Kauzlarich and Kramer (1998a) will be applied to the DynCorp-case with a top-down approach. This model will be used to examine the several linkages between the different catalysts for action on the three levels of analysis. In the first section, the motivational aspects will be analyzed. The second section will focus on the opportunity structure in the DynCorp-case, and the third section will examine the (lack of) effective social control mechanisms. The three different levels of analysis, from institutional to individual, will be processed in all three sections.

© The Author(s) 2018

C. Cole, R. Vermeltfoort, *U.S. Government Contractors and Human Trafficking*, SpringerBriefs in Criminology, https://doi.org/10.1007/978-3-319-70827-0_13

13.1 Motivations

This section examines the possible motivational catalysts for action on the institutional, organizational, and individual level in the DynCorp-case. The motivational factors at the institutional environment will be analyzed from a political economy point of view. Private military companies operate in the broader context of the capitalist society. Within these capitalist societies, a *culture of competition* reflects the pursuit of economic self-interest and strives for success and wealth, which is an inherent characteristic of individuals and organizations (Coleman, 1987). As stated in Chapter 10, one of the biggest differences between a national army and PMSCs is the fact that private military companies are profit-motivated actors. These private military and security companies need to raise money and have to compete with similar organizations in the market for force. On the other hand, the risks of PMSCs to get involved in international crimes may be higher than with other profit-motivated corporations. As noted by Huisman (2010), the risk of involvement in international crimes in the private military industry is connected to the places where the business is to be found. After the war in 1995, BiH was a transitional country with weak police and law enforcement systems. This contextual setting may have increased the likeliness of getting involved in (international) crimes. However, the contract with the US government may have formed an opportunity for huge amounts of profit for DynCorp, which may explain why they deliberately or less deliberately accepted this risk of getting involved in gross human rights abuses. In this sense, the profit motivation may have preponderated the risks of getting involved in (international) crimes.

The profit motivation, at the organizational level, may explain why DynCorp decided to sign the contract despite the risks of getting involved in criminal behavior. However, how can we explain the decision of DynCorp and the US government to knowingly cover up the scandal as this decision made them complicit in the committed crimes? An important motivation for DynCorp's headquarters to cover up the involvement of their personnel in the sex trafficking scene may be the *organizational goal* of loss minimization. When the complicity of DynCorp personnel in gross human rights abuses and its scale would become public, DynCorp could lose its million-dollar contract. Another motivation for the cover up for both DynCorp and the US government may have been damage control and the fundamental desire to protect its own image and legitimacy.

On their website, DynCorp emphasizes the importance of honest, ethical, and legal corporate conduct. The following statement on the core values stems from their codes of conduct (DynCorp International, 2012) and summarizes their view on corporate conduct:

> At DynCorp International it is our commitment to conduct business honestly, ethically and in accordance with best practices and the applicable laws of the U.S. and other countries in which we operate. We are guided at all times by the highest standards of integrity, whether dealing with customers, co-workers or others.

However, as noted by Perrow (1961), there is difference between official goals, as the ones stated in the code of conduct, and the operative culture. Whereas official goals reflect the general purpose of the corporation as presented in official documents and statements, the operative culture constitutes the actual operating policies of the corporation. It is reasonable to think that the operative culture of DynCorp during the UNMBIH, which was not honest, ethical, or in accordance with any law, was guided by loss minimization as the corporation found itself in a situation wherein it could lose its billion-dollar contract. This discrepancy is also reflected in the subunit between the official mandate and the operative culture of the IPTF during the UNMBIH. Security Council Resolution 1088 expanded the IPTF mandate in December 1996 to include investigations of human rights abuses by law enforcement personnel. It was the task of the IPTF to supervise internal investigations of the local police and to ensure that complicit and corrupt officers faced disciplinary and if necessary criminal proceedings. However, the Human Rights Watch report (2002) shows that in reality the work of IPTF monitors had little effect on internal local police investigations. The operative goals of the subunit to maintain good relations with the local police and to close cases, in combination with the high turnover among IPTF monitors, thwarted the monitors to supervise investigations and often discarded follow-up investigations on existing cases (Human Rights Watch, 2002). This shows that the transformation of DynCorp's official goals into an operative criminogenic culture is something that originates in the subunit and cannot be explained by top-down mechanisms stemming from the corporate headquarters.

On the individual level, personal gain may have been an important *individual goal* to participate in the mission in the first place. The majority of DynCorp employees during the mission had never seen paychecks higher than 20,000 dollar per year, whereas they would earn 85,000 dollars during the 1-year mission in BiH (Bolkovac & Lynn, 2011). As trafficking constitutes a property crime, this profit motivation may even explain why DynCorp personnel decided to participate in trafficking, as some of them received money from traffickers in exchange for protection (Human Rights Watch, 2002). In addition, former DynCorp employee Kathryn Bolkovac mentions sexual need as a motivational factor for rape in an isolated environment far away from home (Interview Bolkovac, 2014).

Whereas motivational factors on the macro and meso level, such as the culture of competition and organizational goals, may be able to explain why DynCorp's headquarters and the US government decided to cover up the scandal, it is not sufficient in explaining the widespread transformation process of DynCorp employees from peacekeepers into perpetrators in the host country. In addition, the operative goals of the subunit to maintain good relations with the local police and to close cases may explain why DynCorp employees facilitated the crimes by turning a blind eye, but it cannot explain the etiology of the transformation process into principal perpetrators of the crimes. On the individual level, sexual need and profit maximization may have some validity in explaining why individual employees participated in the trafficking of women and girls in isolated cases. However, these individual motivational factors cannot explain why the transformation into perpetrators was so widespread among a vast group of DynCorp employees. Different group mechanisms that can facilitate and influence the motives to participate in sex trafficking will be discussed in the next section.

13.2 Opportunity Structure

After having discussed the motivational aspects in the previous section, this section examines the opportunity structure of the means that DynCorp used on the institutional, organizational, and individual level to achieve its goals. As described in the previous chapters, DynCorp's main goals consisted of profit maximization and loss minimization on the meso level and closing cases and maintaining good relations with the local police on the individual level. A common proposition in the literature on organizational crime is that if (legal) means to achieve the organizations goals are unavailable on the institutional level, it is more likely that illegal means will be created on the corporate level (Kramer & Michalowski, 1990). This top-down approach is also reflected in the integrated theoretical model on state-corporate crime. The model emphasizes how opportunity structures on the macro level could facilitate the creation of illegal means on the meso level, which in turn influences the perception of availability of illegal means on the micro level. This paragraph examines to what extent the transformation process of DynCorp employees into perpetrators could be explained by the examination of the opportunity structures with this top-down approach. Consequently, this section starts with the examination of the opportunity structure on the macro level.

Under the terms of the Dayton Peace Agreement, the employees of DynCorp were given absolute immunity from criminal prosecution during the UNMBIH. During the mission the DynCorp employees had the same status as UN officials as outlined in Section 18 and 19 of the 1946 Convention on the Privileges and Immunities of the UN (Dayton Peace Agreement, 1995). This type of immunity is equivalent to the immunity of diplomats than to the functional immunity of experts during a mission. This absolute immunity on the macro level provided an important opportunity to adhere to illegal means for the individuals in the host country as they were excused from criminal prosecution and could not be arrested or detained within BiH. Without a waiver of immunity from the UN secretary-general, employees of DynCorp could never face charges in Bosnian courts (Human Rights Watch, 2002). Therefore, removal from service and repatriation were the ultimate sanctions against DynCorp employees during the UNMBIH. This pre-given fact of absolute immunity may have increased the perceptions of availability of illegal means for the individuals in the host country. As noted by former DynCorp employee Bolkovac (Interview, 2014), "when you are 5000 miles away from home and guys are complicit in the sex trafficking industry and get away with it, then hey it might be fun to get away with it too." Even though this pre-given fact of absolute immunity may have increased the perceptions of availability of illegal means for the individuals in the host country, it is not sufficient in explaining why the headquarters of DynCorp created illegal means. In the DynCorp-case, the creation of illegal means by DynCorp in the home state consists of their decision to knowingly cover up the widespread involvement of their personnel in a human trafficking scene. Since the cover-up forms a reaction to the crimes of sex trafficking, it did not create an opportunity for onset but for continuation of these crimes. This decision to cover up the scandal cannot be explained by the availability of illegal means, in the form of absolute immunity, on the institutional level. In this regard, motivation and opportunity depend on each other. Even when there is an opportunity to act in a certain way, a corporation still needs the motivation to act in this particular direction. The motivation to create illegal means on the corporate level was not derived from the institutional level but was influenced by factors within the subunit in the host country. This bottom-up mechanism cannot be analyzed with the original theoretical framework, as this model solely examines top-down mechanisms. This shortcoming of the original model and the explanatory power of bottom-up mechanisms for state-corporate crimes will be discussed in the next chapter.

In addition to absolute immunity as a top-down mechanism, the political environment in BiH may have influenced the decisions of individual DynCorp employees in the host country and their perceptions of its illicit activities. In 1995, when DynCorp entered the country, BiH was a developing country with weak police and law enforcement systems. DynCorp employees had to operate within a situation where traffickers and corrupt local police had little fear for criminal prosecution or punishment as trafficking laws went largely unenforced (Human Rights Watch, 2002). Local prosecutors did not endorse the seriousness of sex trafficking, which resulted in a lack of domestic legal protections for the victims of these serious crimes. Despite available evidence and victims ready to testify, local prosecutors refused to handle a sex trafficking case. According to Celhia de Lavarene, director of the Special Trafficking Operations Program (STOP), prosecutors did not want to talk about human trafficking (Human Rights Watch, 2002). She explains that they only wanted to talk about prostitution, as this is an illegal practice in Bosnia and Herzegovina. This led to a situation in which the Bosnian government only sporadically prosecuted traffickers but occasionally prosecuted victims for prostitution, illegal migration status offenses, and document fraud (Human Rights Watch, 2002). In addition, the Bosnian government largely ignored corruption among local authorities and police and rarely investigated or prosecuted officials for their involvement in the human trafficking scene. This combination of outright corruption, state incompetence, and lack of political will enabled sex-traffickers to violate the law with impunity (Blaustein, 2012). Both on the organizational and the individual level, the perception of the availability and attractiveness of illegal opportunities is very important in the transformation process of peacekeepers into perpetrators. It is possible to argue that the political environment in BiH influenced the attitudes and perceptions of DynCorp employees during the UNMBIH. The already existing and "tolerated" sex trafficking scene may have decreased the *obstacles or constraints* for individual employees in BiH to turn to *illegal means* by getting complicit in the sex trafficking scene.

According to Coleman (1987), the attractiveness of illegal opportunities is determined by four factors: (1) the perception of the potential risks, (2) the perception of the expected gain, (3) the evaluation of other legal opportunities of which the organization is aware, and (4) the compatibility of the opportunity with rationalizations, ideas, and beliefs of the organization. As trafficking constitutes a property crime and the cover-up can be viewed as a form of white-collar crime, Coleman's criteria might have some explanatory power for these two crimes. The expected gain for the principal perpetrators of trafficking in the host state consisted of profit maximization. In addition, for the employees who covered up the involvement of DynCorp personnel and the local police, the expected gain comprised good relations with the local police and the quick closing of cases. On a meso level, the corporations' expected gain for their attempt to cover the scandal up was evading the loss of the million-dollar contract. As noted in this section, the potential risks of illegal opportunities for DynCorp employees in the host country were low during the UNMBIH due to their absolute immunity from criminal prosecution. However, this reasoning is not applicable on the risk perceptions of DynCorp in the home state. The corporate headquarters knew that covering up the scandal brings the potential risk of being caught for this illegal action, which could damage its image and legitimacy. However, the status of force agreement (SOFA), an agreement between the UN and the host country, which effectively prohibited the host country to prosecute DynCorp employees (Human Rights Watch, 2002), lowered this potential risk of getting caught for the cover-up. Former DynCorp employee Kathryn Bolkovac explains that DynCorp, in order to save face, public embarrassment, or repercussions, simply fired those employees who would increase the risk of getting caught (Interview, 2014). Instead of the UN waiving the immunity of the perpetrators and requiring an independent investigation, these contractors typically fall under the same status of force agreement that enables the case to be lost in the gaps provided by these agreements. Bolkovac notes that there is no real intention or way for the UN to do the investigation, because the home countries have the responsibility of disciplinary action or any prosecution that might take place. Ultimately, DynCorp had the final word, as they became this chain of command. Bolkovac explains that this chain of command enabled DynCorp to cover up these cases. However, command structure also worked well for the UN, as it gave them an out. The UN could just say "they took care of it, no evidence was found, we do not know what happened." As Bolkovac notes (Interview, 2014), "it was really convenient and it worked both ways." With regard to the fourth factor, how can we explain that employees adhered to illegal means even though the use of the illegal opportunity was not compatible with rationalizations, ideas, and beliefs of the organization? It is possible to argue that lack of potential risks and promising perceptions of expected gain created a discrepancy between "formal goals" and the operative culture of the corporation, as noted above.

In addition, recruits with low moral standards in the host country may more easily adhere to illegal means, even though these illegal opportunities are not compatible with the ideas and beliefs of the corporation. As noted by Bolkovac (2014), "the recruitment standards of the corporate contractors were not good. They recruited people who should not have been going as representatives of our government. They are lacking all types of things such as advanced education, and understanding of the importance of exemplary codes of conduct and ethics and moral values. Contractors as well as our militaries represent our countries. Many of the people who were recruited for DynCorp were on the last days of being a police officer, they were ready to retire or some of them were ready to be fired from their police forces for conduct and becoming. Some had actually been fired for such charges as sexual harassment against women, and were then hired by DynCorp to go to missions like Bosnia. Therefore, there was an array of issues that many of these recruits already had on their record, who than either applied to work for DynCorp knowing that they could make a lot of money or are recruited because they have a friend who did it. So, the background investigations and vetting processes were really flawed." The fact that DynCorp was responsible for the selection process of new recruits could have created the opportunity to hire friends and fellows prepared to participate in the sex trafficking scene or at least contribute to the cover-up.

13.3 Operationality of Control

Now that we have discussed the motivations and the structures of opportunity, this section will discuss the final catalyst for action, the (lack of) operationality of social control mechanisms. These mechanisms exercise pressure on corporations and its employees to operate by legal means and monitor whether the goals have been achieved in an ethical and legal way. This section will analyze to what extent the widespread transformation process of DynCorp employees into perpetrators may have been influenced by various forms of (lack of) social control mechanisms on the three levels of analysis. While the social control mechanisms on the macro level will be regarded external social controls, the mechanisms on the meso and micro level will be regarded internal social controls.

In 2000, DynCorp faced intense media scrutiny when headlines and news items revealed that a vast majority of DynCorp employees were actively participating in a billion-dollar sex trafficking industry. Once the scandal became world news, DynCorp decided to resign some of their employees under suspicion of illegal activity. However, until that moment there were no external pressures as social control mechanisms affecting DynCorp and their decision making. *Political pressure* remained absent as the US government was complicit in the attempt to cover up the involvement of peacekeepers in the sex trafficking industry. In addition, legal sanctions could not be used as a pressure mechanism as DynCorp possessed absolute immunity during the UNMBIH. Even today, almost 20 years after the scandal, none of the perpetrators have been prosecuted. In fact, DynCorp is still receiving million-dollar contracts, and even today DynCorp employees guilty of participating in the sex trafficking network in BiH are still working as peacekeepers on other missions around the globe (Bolkovac & Lynn, 2011). One could conclude that lack of social control mechanisms on the macro level, such as legal and political pressures, left DynCorp quite unaffected.

On the meso level, a possible internal control mechanism for a corporation in general is (the implementation of) a code of conduct. As noted by Kaptein and Wempe (2002), a code of conduct is a policy document that defines the conduct the corporation expects of its employees and/or the responsibilities of the company toward its stakeholders. The code elucidates the objectives of the corporation, its accountability, and its values and norms. Codes of conduct aim to improve the extent to which the expectations of the corporation's stakeholders are realized, to reduce the occurrence of incidents, to encourage the authorities to relax controls and regulations, and to boost the confidence within the corporation (Kaptein, 2004). As noted earlier in this chapter, DynCorp has been strongly oriented toward honest, ethical, and legal corporate conduct. In mid-1999, before the DynCorp scandal became public, the UN enunciated a "zero tolerance policy" on human trafficking, which was also applicable on DynCorp employees during the UNMBIH. In addition, in November 2000, Pascal Budge, site manager for DynCorp, sent an internal memorandum to all DynCorp officers in the IPTF reporting a rise in disciplinary repatriations related to trafficking in persons and prostitution. The memorandum noted that the repatriations were "embarrassing" and enunciated a "zero tolerance policy" that prohibited DynCorp employees to visit the nightclubs (Human Rights Watch, 2002). However, these rules and standards did not prevent or stop the complicity of DynCorp employees in the sex trafficking scene during the UNMBIH. Apparently, the code of conduct and zero tolerance policy were not successful social control mechanisms for DynCorp employees situated in the difficult political environment in BiH. During the UNMBIH these internal norms were not even carried out by some high-ranking officials in the host country, as they were the ones publicly buying and raping women and girls. Kevin Werner, former DynCorp employee, explains to Human Rights Watch (2002) that he received a videotape that documented his boss, John Hirtz, raping a young white female. The Human Rights Watch report (2002) describes the rape as follows:

> *The encounter displayed John Hirtz engaging in sexual intercourse with a white female. During the encounter the male leaves the view of the camera and returns with what seemed to be a bottle of oil. At the time the male returns to the bed, where the female was located, the female sees the bottle and tells the male "no" numerous times. The male gives her a reply and begins to have intercourse with the female again.*

Madeleine Rees, the director of the UN Human Rights Office in Sarajevo from 1998 to 2006, notes that it is all a question of leadership, as DynCorp employees are militaries (Interview Rees, 2014). "An important act is to enforce. If you have a zero-tolerance policy and then you are weak, then everybody knows that it is not going to be taken seriously. Especially when you, as a leader, are known as one of the perpetrators that is visiting the brothels." As described by Kaptein et al. (2003), the effectiveness and success of a code of conduct does not solely depend on its content but is determined by successful implementation and its process. The behavior of the corporation's high-ranking officials in this process is critical; without considerable effort of officers at the top, the code of conduct is destined to fail. When high-ranking officers do not confirm the code of conduct, as was the case within DynCorp during the UNMBIH, it displays the wrong signal to its employees and loses its credibility. In summary, one could conclude that there clearly was a lack of social control mechanisms in the DynCorp-case, both on the institutional and organizational level. This lack may have facilitated the widespread transformation process of DynCorp employees into perpetrators of sex trafficking.

However, even in the absence of effective social control mechanisms on the macro and meso level, on the individual level, psychological social control mechanisms practically always remain to exist in persons. On the micro level, the emphasis is on explaining the transformation process of DynCorp officers into perpetrators in terms of personality or psychological adjustment. As noted by Smeulers and Grünfeld (2011), the transformation process of an ordinary citizen into a perpetrator of international crimes consists of three phases, namely, the (1) preparation phase, (2) the initiation phase, and (3) the routinization/habituation phase. In the first phase, the preparation phase, individuals submit themselves to an organizational culture and structure or a collective identity. The initiation phase reflects the gradual involvement in crimes. In this phase, individuals have to consciously or unconsciously reduce their moral inhibitions, as they need to be psychologically prepared to harm other individuals. Habituation, in the routinization/habituation phase, is the phenomenon in which individuals come to see the familiar as automatically good.

In the DynCorp-case, the submission to a collective identity of being a DynCorp officer during the UNMBIH could have been facilitated by the fact that they came a long way and were isolated in an environment with no social life, except their colleagues. An important mechanism in this context is *conformity to the group.* As noted by Aronson (2004), individuals are "social animals" and like to conform to a group and its norms because of fear of being rejected and group pressure. Groups define our identity, and adhering to it leads to acceptance and respect of others. Due to these group dynamics, it requires a lot of courage to exert control on the behavior of what seems to be the vast majority of the corporation. Madeleine Rees, Head of the UN Office of the High Commissionaire for Human Rights in BiH, explains the power of male bonding for the transformation process of DynCorp employees into perpetrators during the UNMBIH. "Never underestimate the power of male bonding. There are coming many men from many different countries, from Africa, Asia as well as Europeans. There is nothing to do. They feel that it is ok, that it is right, that it is part of male privilege. This is how pack mentality develops. You are isolated, you are in a place where you do not speak the language, where you do not know anybody and your male buddies are your family. Are you going to stand up against what seems to be the majority, the vast majority will not. Even though they are probably the majority themselves and they are wrong, they do not want to be the one who says that. So it ends up with a self-perpetuating dynamic in itself" (Interview Rees, 2014). This statement reflects that there were masculine ways of *groupthink,* which was hard to escape as an individual. The sociologist Flood (2008) examined the dangers of homosocial collectivity with regard to sexual violence. The sociologist explains how heterosexual sex forms a means to status and masculine affirmation. He argues (2008, p. 13) that "male bonding feeds sexual violence against women and sexual violence against women feeds male bonding." In line with this reasoning, Scully (1990) mentions that rape can be practiced as an expression of and as a means to male bonding. It is possible to argue that there was a strong sense of homosocial collectivity within the subunit of DynCorp, as the subunit was predominantly masculine and homosocial. In addition, the involvement of high-ranking officials in the trafficking scene may have facilitated this homosocial collectivity within the subunit. Madeleine Rees (Interview, 2014) mentions that the ones in position of command thought it were just a bunch of whores, who were making money of the troops. The final word of those in command was that boys will be boys and that they will not dictate the morality. Rees notes, "once you have that as an argument it is very difficult to address the issue."

Once individuals submit themselves to an organizational culture or collective identity, they have to reduce their moral inhibitions in the initiation phase, in order to be morally prepared to harm others. Despite powerful group dynamics, individuals often remain to experience *cognitive dissonance* (Festinger, 1957). This concept describes the uncomfortable feeling that individuals experience when one's opinion and behavior do not match with each other. When it is the behavior that causes the divergence, it is easier to change the mindset than to change the behavior. The moral disengagement that follows to change the mindset consists of psychological maneuvers that can selectively disengage moral restraints from violent conduct (Bandura, 1999). Criminologists Matza and Sykes (1957) examined these neutralization techniques with respect to "ordinary crime." They argue that when individuals commit illegitimate acts, they must employ neutralization techniques to silence the "inner voice" of moral self-sanctions. In line with Matza and Sykes, Coleman (1987) notes in the context of white-collar crime that neutralization techniques are not solely applied after the law is violated but might as well be used before the act has taken place. In this regard, the use of neutralization techniques may have formed an integral part of the motivation toward illegitimate behavior for DynCorp employees. One of the neutralization techniques that may have formed an integral part of the motivation of DynCorp employees to participate in crimes was the denial of victim. The perpetrators' view of the people they mistreat is a determinative factor for the strength of moral self-censure (Bandura, 1999). As Madeleine Rees (Interview, 2014) notes, "everyone, from the lower ranking officers to the ones in command thought it were just a bunch of whores down there who were making money of the troops." The fact that DynCorp employees regarded the trafficked women and girls as just a bunch of whores instead of human trafficking victims may have weakened their moral self-censure for the cruel conduct. Once the transformation process was put in motion, neutralization techniques may have served as justifications for the illegal acts. A powerful mechanism to cognitively restructure harmful conduct is *advantageous comparison*. Bandura (1999) mentions in this regard that the way behavior is viewed is colored by what it is compared against. As noted by Kathryn Bolkovac (Interview, 2014), some of the complicit DynCorp employees really believed that buying girls and keeping them for themselves in their homes was the right thing to do. They felt like the hero, because they saved her from the abusive environment or stated that they are better off doing this than they are in their home countries. Through advantageous comparison with the actions of the traffickers or the situation in the home country of the women and girls, these DynCorp employees may have convinced themselves that their actions prevented more harm than they would cause.

Coleman's (1987) neutralization techniques are applicable on a broad range of illicit behavior of (employees of) corporations. Criminologist Huisman (2008) specified Coleman's (1987) neutralization techniques even further in order to apply the theory on a more specific type of organizational crime, namely, corporate involvement in international crimes. Huisman (2008) argues that many of Coleman's techniques may be useful when trying to understand corporate involvement in international crimes. One of the neutralization techniques, as mentioned by Coleman (1987), that can both be used before and after the illegitimate behavior is transformation of responsibility. According to Huisman (2008), corporations may reason that their behavior is normal in operating countries by using the argument of "everybody does it." This way of reasoning replaces the responsibility from an individual to a larger group. Another way of transforming responsibility is by claiming that others considered the acts acceptable. The reasoning behind this psychological maneuver is that when an individual conforms to the expectation of others, the offender is not responsible for the actions himself. In addition, corporations might argue that rules are lacking in the host country, so that the corporation cannot break any. It is possible to argue that in the DynCorp-case, these neutralization techniques were used as there were no rules regarding sex trafficking and there was an overall feeling of "everybody does it." All these psychological maneuvers may have reduced the moral inhibitions of DynCorp employees in the initiation phase, which made them morally prepared to harm others. In addition, psychologist Aronson (2004) states that the feeling of cognitive dissonance depends on whether important elements of one's self-concept, such as high moral standards, are being threatened. Therefore, individuals with lower moral standards experience less cognitive dissonance when committing illegitimate acts than individuals with high moral standards. It may be argued that DynCorp employees in BiH needed less psychological maneuvers to be morally prepared to harm others, as the vast majority of the recruits, as stated in the paragraph on motivation, lacked understanding of the importance of exemplary codes of conduct, ethics, and moral values.

Moreover, justification for illegal behavior from above leads to perceived authorization on the micro level (Kelman, 2005). Former DynCorp employee, Kathryn Bolkovac, describes how complicity of high-ranking officials on the meso level could have led to perceived authorization of the behavior by lower-ranking officials. "The eyes were shut and it was condoned and facilitated from above. In other words, they were just as participatory as the lower level officers. They were having women brought into their personal homes, to parties, sending private diplomatic cars to pick up women. So you could say that the behavior was condoned and authorized from above" (Interview Bolkovac, 2014). In this sense these crimes may be regarded as crimes of obedience. According to Kelman (2005), we can speak of a crime of obedience when a crime takes place, not in opposition of the authorities, but in an environment in which such acts are implicitly sponsored, expected, or at least tolerated by the authorities. Moreover, the role of authorization is strengthened when employees are acting within a hierarchy in which they are expected to obey (Kelman, 2005). As noted by Madeleine Rees (Interview, 2014), DynCorp employees are militaries trained to follow leadership. We could argue that, within this hierarchical atmosphere in which high-ranking officials set the bad example, compliant behavior was hard to demand from the lower-ranking employees.

13.4 Summary

This chapter analyzed to what extent the widespread transformation process of DynCorp employees into perpetrators of human trafficking and endeavoring a cover-up during the UNMBIH can be explained by the original theory and framework of state-corporate crime. This multidimensional theory and model was used to examine the linkages between three catalysts for action on three levels of analysis with a top-down approach in the DynCorp-case.

The first section of this chapter examined the motivational factors on the institutional, organizational, and individual level. The contextual setting of BiH as a transitional and weak country may have increased the likeliness for corporations to get involved in international crimes when operating in the country. The combination of profit motivation and a culture of competition surrounding PMSCs in capitalist societies may explain why DynCorp deliberately or less deliberately accepted this risk by signing the contract in the first place. The decision of the corporate headquarters, on the meso level, to cover the scandal up may be explained by the organizational goal of loss minimization. In fact, when the complicity of DynCorp personnel in the sex trafficking scene would become public, DynCorp could lose its million-dollar contract. On the individual level, the isolated acts of rape and trafficking may be explained by the respective individual goals of sexual need and profit maximization. However, these factors cannot explain why the transformation process was so widespread among a vast group of DynCorp employees in the host country.

The second section analyzed the opportunity structure of means as the second catalyst for action. In the DynCorp-case, absolute immunity on the macro level provided an important opportunity to adhere to and increased perceptions of the availability of illegal means on the individual level. In addition, the political environment in BiH with an already existing and tolerated sex trafficking scene may have decreased the obstacles and constraints for individual employees to turn to illegal means. The combination of low perceptions of potential risks, high perceptions of expected gain, and low moral standards may have increased the attractiveness of illegal means on the individual level.

The third section discussed the last catalyst for action, namely, the (lack of) social control mechanisms. One the macro level, lack of legal and political pressures left DynCorp quite unaffected. In addition, the combination of an unsuccessful implementation and process of the code of conduct and high-ranking officials setting a bad example on the meso level may have facilitated the transformation process of DynCorp employees into perpetrators during the UNMBIH. On the individual level, moral inhibitions to use violence may have been reduced by groupthink, conformity to the group, moral disengagement, and the use of neutralization techniques. Moreover, the complicity of high-ranking officials on the meso level may have led to perceived authorization of the behavior on the individual level.

Chapter 14
Revised Analytical Framework

The former chapter applied Kauzlarich and Kramer's theoretical framework on the DynCorp case and analyzed the extent of its explanatory power for the widespread transformation process of DynCorp employees during the UNMBIH. While the framework, by examining the key factors with a top-down approach on the intersections of the catalysts for action and levels of analysis, may have some validity in explaining the crimes, this chapter argues that the original model tends to overlook important explanatory processes and mechanisms for the transformation process. The current chapter tries to answer the second part of the main research question as stated in the introduction of this thesis and analyses to what extent the transformation of DynCorp employees can be explained by subunit analysis and a bidirectional (top-down and bottom-up) approach. The first section of this chapter will outline the shortcomings of Kauzlarich and Kramer's model in explaining the transformation process of DynCorp employees into perpetrators of sex trafficking and endeavoring a cover-up for these crimes. The second section substantiates the power of subunit analysis and a bidirectional approach when examining the crimes and presents a revised analytical framework. The last section summarizes the results of this chapter.

14.1 Shortcomings of State-Corporate Crime Theory

The theoretical model of state-corporate crime examines explanatory factors on three levels of analysis, namely, the institutional, organizational, and individual level. Due to this threefold division, state-corporate crime theory tries to explain corporate criminal behavior by focusing on the corporation as a whole. When applying state-corporate crime theory on the criminal behavior of PMSCs, both the headquarters in the home state and the subunits in the host state will be merged into one level of analysis. Even though PMSCs can be seen as one corporation, there is often a major difference between the environment and manner of involvement in crimes

© The Author(s) 2018

C. Cole, R. Vermeltfoort, *U.S. Government Contractors and Human Trafficking*, SpringerBriefs in Criminology, https://doi.org/10.1007/978-3-319-70827-0_14

of the headquarters and the subunit in the host country. The previous chapter showed that these major differences in environment and manner of involvement were also present in the DynCorp case. Whereas the subunit was situated in a transitional state with weak law enforcement and police systems, the headquarters operated from a distance within a capitalist society. In addition to the environment, there were also major differences between the headquarters and the subunit of DynCorp with regard to the manners of involvement in the crimes. The manner of involvement of DynCorp personnel in the host state can be divided in two groups, namely, principal perpetrators and complicit perpetrators. Whereas the principal perpetrators raped and trafficked girls and women, the complicit perpetrators knowingly decided to turn a blind eye. As former DynCorp employee Kathryn Bolkovac (Interview, 2014) notes, "there was a large group of DynCorp officers who were not having sex with these girls, but were going to these bars watching them dance, knowing that colleagues were doing this and said nothing. Through true ignorance they facilitated the crimes. They were in a sense just as bad by covering up the issue." The manner of involvement of DynCorp in the home state is comparable to the group of facilitating perpetrators in the host state. However, the headquarters of DynCorp operated from a distance and became complicit in a later stage when they facilitated the crimes by covering the scandal up. A shortcoming of state-corporate crime theory, and therefore of the model, is that merging the headquarters and the subunit into one level of analysis tends to overlook these major differences in operational environments and manners of involvement in the crimes. An additional shortcoming of regarding the corporation as one level of analysis in the theory and the model is that it impedes the examination of processes and mechanisms between the corporate headquarters and the subunit that may create and facilitate the criminogenic environment.

Another weakness is that the explanatory power of both the theory and the model solely rests on top-down mechanisms, whereby institutional factors influence the choices of corporations, which in turn determine the behavior of individuals within the corporation. The timeline of the crimes in the DynCorp case, on the other hand, shows that the crimes do not originate in the institutional or organizational level, but within the subunit in the host state. In fact, the type of crime changed over time. In an early stage, one could argue that the involvement of isolated DynCorp employees in the trafficking scene, which were participatory for their own benefit and without support of the corporation, could be viewed as occupational crime. However, as substantiated in previous chapters, as the organization provided the opportunity structures and lack of social control mechanisms that facilitated (the complicity in) sex trafficking, the committed crimes in the DynCorp case can be conceptualized as organizational crime. Due to the inter-organizational relationships between DynCorp's headquarters and the US government and the decision of both actors to endeavor a cover-up instead of taking disciplinary actions, one could speak of state-corporate crime. Even though the original model with a top-down approach may have some validity in explaining the origin and further effects of the opportunity structure and (lack of) social control mechanisms in the DynCorp case, it cannot fully explain the hybrid mixture of crimes within and the etiology of the transformation process of DynCorp employees into perpetrators during the UNMBIH. The fact that the complicity in crimes originated in the subunit makes it impossible to explain the motivational, opportunity, and social control factors for the transformation process by solely focusing on top-down mechanisms. The next section will substantiate the power of subunit analysis with a bidirectional approach, which examines both top-down and bottom-up mechanisms. The section moreover presents a revised analytical framework, which tries to rectify the raised deficiencies of the original model.

14.2 The Power of Subunit Analysis and a Bidirectional Approach

The previous paragraph substantiated the shortcomings of state-corporate crime theory and the associated theoretical model in explaining the transformation process of DynCorp officers into perpetrators in BiH. The main limitations of the theory and model are that it tends to overlook important processes and mechanisms by merging both the headquarters and the subunit into one level of analysis and by solely examining top-down mechanisms. This section presents a revised analytical framework, which tries to rectify these limitations by expanding the theory to incorporate the subunit as a separate level of analysis. This additional level will be placed between the organizational level, which represents the headquarters, and the individual level. Adding the subunit as a separate level of analysis enables us to examine the catalysts for action of the subunit, separately from those of the headquarters in the home state, in explaining the transformation process of DynCorp employees. It moreover enables us to examine the complex mechanisms and interrelationships between the headquarters and the subunit that may have created and facilitated DynCorp's criminogenic environment. The revised analytical framework endorses that the explanatory power of the transformation process rests not solely on top-down, but also on bottom-up mechanisms. In fact, this bottom-up approach enables us to explain how factors in the subunit may influence the decisions of corporations, which in turn may influence decisions of the state. As noted by former DynCorp employee Kathryn Bolkovac (Interview, 2014), "it was the abuse of power and authority in the host state that enabled institutional abuses to take place."

The key factors on the subunit level of analysis will be adopted from Braithwaite's integrated organizational crime theory (1989). This theory integrated mainstream theories as labeling theory, opportunity theory, control theory, and subcultural theory in order to understand the circumstances that lead to organizational crime. The main argument of Braithwaite's theory (1989) is that organizational crime is more likely to occur when subcultures of resistance to law are strong. Powerful subunits are able to neutralize the moral bond to law, transmit knowledge on how to create illegitimate opportunities, and secure these opportunities by covering up the offending (Braithwaite, 1989). The implementation of Braithwaite's theory into the original theoretical framework for state-corporate crime is displayed in Table 14.1.

Table 14.1 An integrated theoretical model of state-corporate crime (revised)

Level of analysis	Motivation	Opportunity structure	Operationality of control
Institutional environment	Culture of competition Economic pressure Organizational goals Performance	Availability of legal means Obstacles and constraints Blocked goals/strain Availability of illegal means Access to resources	International reactions Political pressure Legal sanctions Media scrutiny Public opinion Social movements
Organizational	Corporate culture Operative goals	Instrumental rationality Internal constraint Creation of illegal means Role specialization Task segregation Communication technologies Normalization of violence	Culture of compliance Codes of conduct Reward structure Safety and quality control procedures Communication processes
Subunit	Subunit goals Managerial pressure	Available illegitimate opportunities Transmitting knowledge Definitions of situations	Concerned ignorance Informal social control Differential shaming Organizational complexity
Interaction	Socialization Social meaning Individual goals Competitive individualism Material success emphasis	Perception of availability and attractiveness of illegal means	Personal morality Rationalizations and techniques of neutralization Separation from consequences Obedience to authority Group think Diffusion of responsibility

Within the revised analytical framework, the *subunit goals* in the first catalyst for action are transferred from the organizational to the subunit level. In addition, the motivational factor *managerial pressure* is replaced from the headquarters to the subunit, as managerial pressure derives from the organizational level and may vertically influence the motivation of employees in the subunits. These motivating factors of subunit goals and managerial pressure in the DynCorp case were discussed in the previous chapter. As noted by Braithwaite (1989), different factors can facilitate the creation and continuation of crime within organizations. These facilitating factors can be subscribed under opportunity structure and (lack of) operationality of control.

Under opportunity structure, the original model of state-corporate crime mentions the availability of legal and illegal means on the institutional level and the creation of illegal means on the organizational level. The associated top-down mechanism explicates how lack of legal means and the availability of illegal means on the institutional level could lead to the creation of illegal means on the organizational level. However, in the DynCorp case, the decision to cover up the scandal, as the creation of illegal means on the organizational level, cannot solely be explained by top-down mechanisms originating in the institutional level. The pre-given fact that DynCorp employees possessed absolute immunity from criminal prosecution during the UNMBIH may have facilitated the transformation process of DynCorp employees into perpetrators within the subunit. However, the decision of DynCorp's headquarters to cover up the scandal cannot be explained by the presence of this absolute immunity. The explanatory power of the decision to cover up the scandal lies with the *availability of illegitimate opportunities* within the subunit. Cutler (2010) notes in this regard that PMSCs enjoy the so-called first-mover advantage. This phenomenon explains that the first corporation in a transitional and weak state has the ability to influence the regulatory process and to compile it in their own advantage. It is possible to argue that DynCorp possessed this first-mover advantage, as they were (one of) the first corporation(s) that entered BiH after the war. In addition, during the UNMBIH, the main task of DynCorp's subunit was to restructure and reform the local police and monitor their performance, especially on human rights issues (Simic, 2004). It is possible to argue that on the subunit level, the combination of absolute immunity, the first-mover advantage, and the task to restructure the local police provided illegitimate opportunities, which increased the likeliness for DynCorp employees to get involved in the crimes. The widespread involvement of DynCorp employees in sex trafficking throughout the subunit may have triggered the (perceived) blockage of legitimate opportunities of the headquarters in the home state. The legitimate opportunity when the headquarters learned about the widespread involvement of their personnel was to take disciplinary actions against all employees involved in rape and sex trafficking. However, the adherent risk of losing the million-dollar contract may have led to the perceived blockage of this legitimate opportunity. As noted by Huisman (2010), corporations often underestimate the possible risks and costs of their involvement in crimes. The criminologist explains that the fear of losing contracts influences the outcome of risk assessments. In addition, Braithwaite (1989) notes in this regard that PMSCs deal with major win-lose situations as the growth of the corporation depends on a small number of buyers and contracts. The combination of these factors may explain why DynCorp's headquarters decided to knowingly cover up the involvement of their personnel in the sex trafficking scene to safeguard the million-dollar contract. In this regard, the decision to create illegal means on the organizational level was influenced by (lack of) opportunities from both the institutional and subunit level of analysis. In fact, the headquarters of DynCorp literally stood between their subunit and the institutional level and may have been influenced by bidirectional mechanisms in the creation of their illegal means.

Another important factor, as mentioned by Braithwaite (1989), that creates and maintains the illegitimate opportunity structure within subunits is *transmission of knowledge*. The criminologist argues that subunits transmit knowledge on how corporate actors can work together to break the law. The transmission of knowledge could result in rationalizing the behavior as necessary, good, and inevitable. According to Human Rights Watch (2002), widespread corruption throughout the local police in BiH allowed the trafficking scene to flourish. The police directly and indirectly facilitated the trafficking scene by managing nightclubs or as clients of and informants to brothel owners. According to Braithwaite (1989), it is very likely that a corrupt police department transmits the subculture of corruption to its new recruits. The close cooperation between DynCorp personnel and the (corrupt) local police may have facilitated the transmission of knowledge on how the private contractors could play their part in sustaining the illegal opportunity structure. In addition, the ones already serving in BiH could have influenced the new recruits within DynCorp's subunit. Former DynCorp employee Kathryn Bolkovac notes that the presence of young girls in BiH almost became a recruitment tool for DynCorp (Interview, 2014). Bolkovac describes how a person who already served in Bosnia bragged about young, pretty girls during their 1-week training before the mission in BiH. "Even before the mission started there was a guy telling the new recruits that he knew places where you could get nice 12 to 15 year old girls. The guys who were talking like that were the ones who were in the mission before and became the managers of those missions. This attitude absolutely influenced the new recruits, because somebody has to show them the ropes when they get in the country. These new recruits do not just step off a bus and say, 'oh wow, there is a strip club let's go.' Somebody tells them about it."

In addition, the fact that DynCorp personnel worked closely together with the (corrupt) local police may have facilitated the change in *definitions of the situation* within the subunit. As noted by Braithwaite (1989), crime arises within a subunit when definitions unfavorable to law violation are exceeded by definitions favorable to law violation. The definition of human trafficking used by the UNBMIH between 1995 and 2001 contravened and was less strict than the definition in international law as articulated in Article 3 of the Trafficking Protocol (Human Rights Watch, 2002). The report (2002) notes that following the definition used during the UNMBIH, trafficking in human beings consisted of any acts involving:

- The movement, transportation, or recruitment of persons across or within frontiers whether for financial gain or otherwise
- And in which coercion, material deception, force, abuse of authority, direct or indirect threats, fraud, or fraudulent nondisclosure is used
- For the purpose of placing persons against their will, forcibly or without their consent, in abusive, exploitative, or servile situations, such as forced prostitution, domestic servitude, sweatshop labor or other abusive forms of labor, or family relationships whether for pay or not

This definition of human trafficking that was used by the UNMBIH places emphasis on the element of consent of the trafficked person, without giving sufficient consideration to material deception, coercion, and force. Consequently, trafficked victims who knew that they would work in the sex industry were in any case excluded from the definition. However, under international law, no person can consent to debt bondage or being sold as chattel (Human Rights Watch, 2002). As prostitution was an illegal practice in BiH, trafficked women often faced prosecution in local courts themselves instead of being regarded trafficking victims.

DynCorp employees in the host country therefore may have faced a situation in which compliance with international law meant resistance with national law and vice versa. In addition, corruption among the local police and authorities was largely ignored by the Bosnian government (Human Rights Watch, 2002). They rarely investigated, disciplined, or prosecuted corrupt officials for their involvement in the sex trafficking industry. These perspectives and attitudes in the host country could have led to a situation in which definitions unfavorable to (international) law violation are exceeded by definitions favorable to (international) law violation. As compared to their headquarters, DynCorp employees in the host state were embedded in the situational definitions of the host state, because they handed over their cases to the prosecutors of local courts and cooperated with the local police. Former DynCorp employee Kathryn Bolkovac (Interview, 2014) explains that her colleagues perceived the trafficked girls as prostitutes instead of victims. "The good old boys who were doing this work for years grew up with this whole prostitution is prostitution attitude. They think that if a girl is in a house for prostitution or in a brothel she is a prostitute. This is the old school mentality that still exists within these hierarchies in these corporations." Bolkovac moreover describes a conversation with the contingent commander who said things like "well, if these girls really want to leave, then why don't they whisper in our ears that they want to leave when we go into these brothels?" (Interview, 2014). It is possible to argue that this change in definitions, with regard to the practice of human trafficking and its victims, facilitated the transformation process of DynCorp employees within the subunit in the host country during the UNMBIH.

Once criminal subunits are formed, different factors can weaken or strengthen subunits of resistance to law. These social control mechanisms on the subunit level consist of *concerned ignorance*, *informal social control*, *differential shaming*, and *organizational complexity*. According to Braithwaite (1989), subunits of noncompliance with law have a bigger chance to sustain when organizations enforce a code of secrecy. The criminologist notes that criminal organizations have a distinctive nature of *concerned ignorance*, in which sticking your nose in other people's business or internal whistleblowing is a fatal career move. It is possible to argue that this culture of concerned ignorance was also present within DynCorp's subunit during the UNMBIH. As noted by Kathryn Bolkovac (Interview, 2014), "there was an isolated group of individuals who did their very best to cover up what was going on and they had done very well for many years. Then there were other high-level individuals within DynCorp, as well as in the state department and the U.N., who just kind of stood back and decided that removing whistleblowers from the situation was the best way to sustain this code of secrecy. It was what many within DynCorp referred to as an open secret." It is possible to argue that DynCorp, in collaboration with the state department and the UN, sustained the subunit of noncompliance through their attitude of concerned ignorance and the enforcement of a code of secrecy. In addition to concerned ignorance, *organizational complexity* can facilitate the continuation of crime within organizations. The organizational complexity during the UNMBIH is reflected in the fact that there was a mixture of military troops and civilian police from 45 UN countries, with diverse and unclear tasks (Bolkovac and

Lynn, 2011). Only the IPTF, which was staffed by DynCorp employees, consisted of 1411 civilian police officers from all over the world. Former DynCorp employee Kathryn Bolkovac (Interview, 2014) describes that "you could be working for the U.N., DynCorp and the state department at the same time. There was too much overarching supervision, mixed lines of reporting and not enough accountability along those lines." As noted by Braithwaite (1989), organizational complexity can be used to protect individual employees from their own conscience and from shaming by their colleagues with a stronger conscience.

In addition, Braithwaite (1989) mentions *differential shaming* as an important mechanism for informal social control. The criminologist presents differential shaming as a theory of tipping points between two mutually contradictory theories on the effects of informal social control, namely, subcultural theory and control theory. Whereas control theory concerns the exercise of informal social control to secure compliance with law, subcultural theory explicates how informal social control secures noncompliance with law. Braithwaite argues that differential shaming determines when the balance of informal social control favors subcultural theory or control theory. Braithwaite (1989, p. 9) defined shaming as "an expression of disapproval that may be enacted in an infinite variety of verbal and nonverbal cultural forms." The most important forms of shaming occur by the general community or the state in the form of a criminal conviction or within independent groups, such as workmates or family (Braithwaite, 1989). Individuals within criminogenic corporations therefore often experience differential shaming that cuts in opposite directions. They often experience shaming from a majoritarian morality of compliance with law and a subunit's morality of noncompliance with law. Whereas shaming by the general community and the state can be regarded as extra-organizational shaming on the institutional level, shaming by workmates can be seen as shaming on the organizational or subunit level of analysis. In addition, shaming those who defy the norms of criminal subunits strengthens these subunits. Shortly after blowing the whistle on the involvement of her colleagues in the sex trafficking scene, former DynCorp employee Kathryn Bolkovac was fired on the grounds of not completing her time sheets. Bolkovac brought a lawsuit against DynCorp, alleging she was dismissed for investigating the illegal behavior of fellow officers in BiH. In 2001, she won the case. In addition, DynCorp fired another employee right after they found out that he was investigating the sexual misconduct of colleagues. It is possible to argue that the dismissal of two DynCorp employees, who were in compliance with (international) law, strengthened the criminal subunit of noncompliance with (international) law. The intra-organizational shaming, in this regard, may have worked counterproductive as DynCorp shamed those who complied with law, did not "play the game," or blew the whistle to the outside world.

14.3 Summary

This chapter tried to rectify the limitations of state-corporate crime theory and the associated model in explaining the transformation process of DynCorp employees into perpetrators during UNMBIH. The first section of this chapter substantiated the shortcomings of state-corporate crime theory and Kauzlarich and Kramer's model in explaining the transformation process. The main limitations of the theory and the model are that they merge both the headquarters and the subunit into one level of analysis and that they solely examine top-down mechanisms. The second paragraph presented a revised analytical framework, which analyzed whether the implementation of a subunit level of analysis in the original model increased the explanatory power for the transformation during the UNMBIH. The factors on the subunit level of analysis are derived from Braithwaite's (1989) integrated theory of organizational crime, which argues that corporate crime is more likely to occur when subunits of resistance to law are strong. The second section moreover analyzed the power of a bidirectional approach in examining the top-down and bottom-up mechanisms and processes between DynCorp's headquarters and their subunit in BiH. Examining bottom-up mechanisms could explain how the well-intentioned peacekeeping mission in BiH, from both DynCorp and the US government, could turn into involvement in a major sex trafficking scene, because of available illegitimate opportunities and (lack) of social control mechanisms on the subunit level of analysis.

The analysis in this chapter showed that different opportunity structures and social control mechanisms on the subunit level, separately from those at the headquarters, possess explanatory power for the transformation process of DynCorp employees during the UNMBIH. In addition, the analysis showed that the explanatory power of the transformation process does not solely rely on top-down mechanisms, but on bidirectional interrelationships between the headquarters in the home state and the subunit in the host state. In addition to absolute immunity derived from the institutional level, different factors on the subunit level may have created an opportunity structure for the transformation process from peacekeepers into perpetrators. The combination between absolute immunity, the task to restructure and monitor the local police, and the "first-mover advantage" may have provided the illegitimate opportunities for the subunit in the host country to construct the rules in their own advantage. Another factor that may have created and maintained the illegitimate opportunity structure within the subunit is transmission of knowledge, as DynCorp employees in the subunit worked closely together with the corrupt local police. In addition, during the UNMBIH compliance with national law meant resistance with international law as the definition of human trafficking used during the mission contravened the international legal definition. As the employees in the host state worked closely together with the local police and prosecutors, it is possible to argue that this led to a situation in which definitions unfavorable to (international) law violation were exceeded by definitions favorable to (international) law violation. This, in turn, may have facilitated the transformation process during the

UNMBIIH. In addition, organizational complexity, informal social control, and differential shaming may have strengthened the subunits of resistance to (international) law in BiH. The organizational complexity during the UNMBIH may have protected DynCorp employees from both their own conscience and from shaming by colleagues with a stronger conscience. The differential shaming through the dismissal of two DynCorp officers who complied with (international) law could have made the illegitimate subunit even stronger. Another factor that could have sustained the subunit of noncompliance is concerned ignorance and the enforcement of a code of secrecy by the DynCorp's headquarters, the state department, and the UN.

The analysis in Chap. 4 showed that the original theory and model of state-corporate crime, with a top-down approach, has some validity in explaining the origin and further effects of some opportunity structures and (lack of) social control mechanisms in the DynCorp case. However, the original model cannot explain how complex mechanisms and interrelationships between DynCorp's headquarters and their subunit facilitated the transformation process of DynCorp employees into perpetrators during the UNMBIH. Adding the subunit as a separate level of analysis in the revised framework as presented in this chapter enabled us to examine the catalysts for action of the subunit, separately from those of the headquarters in the home state, in explaining the transformation process of DynCorp employees. It moreover enabled us to examine the complex mechanisms and interrelationships between the headquarters and the subunit that may have created and facilitated DynCorp's criminogenic environment. The analysis in this chapter examined how independent factors within the subunit and complex interrelationships between the subunit and DynCorp in the home state could have facilitated the transformation process of DynCorp employees during the UNMBIH.

Chapter 15
Discussion and Recommendations

Chapter 13 of this thesis answered the first part of the main research question as stated in the introduction of this thesis. This chapter substantiated how we can explain the widespread transformation process of DynCorp employees from peacekeepers into perpetrators during the UNMBIH by applying Kauzlarich & Kramer's original theoretical framework of state-corporate crime on the case. Chapter 14 answered the second part of the main research question by examining to what extent this transformation could be explained by subunit analysis and a bidirectional approach. After answering the main research question, also, in Chap. 14, the research and the generalizability of its results were evaluated. Did the research provide possible useful insights for criminology? How? And which recommendations can be given for further research?

In order to answer the main research question, this thesis had to rely on information that could not be provided by (independent) academic scholars. Lack of access to the practices of DynCorp during the UNMBIH and the explorative character of the case study necessitated the use of media articles, NGO reports, and research of supranational organizations. Even though these sources provide a lot of on-the-ground information, the reliability, completeness, and truthfulness of these sources cannot be granted. However, in order to overcome this methodological disadvantage, this thesis attempted to combine as many different sources as possible. In addition, to overcome possible biases and partisanship when interpreting the sources, the researcher tried to remain as objective as possible at every stage of the process by constantly taking distance from the described arguments and by considering possible counterarguments. Even though the best explanation of the transformation process of DynCorp employees may have been obtained by researching the perceptions from a perpetrator's perspective, this was almost impossible due to the sensitivity and accessibility of the subject. In the absence of a perpetrator's perspective, the researcher obtained an understanding of the transformation process by interviewing participants who were situated in the same environment and

© The Author(s) 2018

C. Cole, R. Vermeltfoort, *U.S. Government Contractors and Human Trafficking*, SpringerBriefs in Criminology, https://doi.org/10.1007/978-3-319-70827-0_15

organizational context and therefore subject to the same explanatory factors as the perpetrators during the UNMBIH.

In addition, this thesis relied on literature research, which was examined from a criminological perspective. The explanatory factors for the transformation process of DynCorp employees into perpetrators stemmed from Kauzlarich & Kramer's theoretical framework and Braithwaite's (1989) integrated theory on organizational crime. This thesis analyzed the transformation process during the UNMBIH on four levels of analysis. In addition to a literature study, the researcher also conducted two in-depth interviews with a participant and area expert for on-the-ground information and to substantiate the transformation of the descriptive explanations into analytical explanations.

In recent years more and more cases have come to light in which peacekeepers turn into perpetrators of gross human rights abuses, namely, in Haiti, Sudan, the Democratic Republic of the Congo, and Kosovo. The involvement in international crimes affects the legitimacy of the (private) military and security industry, including peacekeepers, private contractors, and in some cases even the UN. These alarming developments certify the societal relevance of examining the transformation process of peacekeepers into perpetrators of crimes. When PMSCs would endorse that powerful subunits in the host state may increase the likelihood of involvement in crimes, they may more critically reflect on how their decisions and behavior can foster subunits of resistance to law. In addition, the empirical findings of the detailed examination of the case study contributed to theory building and refinement, which reflects the academic relevance of this thesis. This thesis rendered useful theoretical insights for criminology in general and for complicity of PMSCs in (international) crimes in specific. This thesis examined the case study with a deviant approach, as there are no theories in the literature that examine the power of subunits with both a top-down and bottom-up approach within the bigger macro, meso, and micro context. Through the analysis of a case that fails to fit existing theories, this thesis developed a new theory by inductively identifying new variables and causal mechanisms. However, even though the intensive study of the DynCorp case provided significant theoretical insights into the power of subunits and a bidirectional approach in this specific case, we must be careful with generalizing the results to other cases of state-corporate crime. The fact that this research only examined one case within the specific area of PMSC criminality limits the generalizability of the results.

However, this research may have some effect on the applicability of the contemporary theory of state-corporate crime on cases of PMSC criminality. The research showed that, even though the complicity of DynCorp in sex trafficking and endeavoring a cover-up of this crime can be regarded a state-corporate crime, the theory and its associated theoretical model are not sufficient in explaining these crimes. In fact, by merging both the subunit and headquarters in one level of analysis, the theory tends to overlook the differences in environment, manner of involvement in crimes, and the mechanisms between the corporate headquarters and the subunit. It is possible to argue that these limitations also hamper the explanation of other cases of PMSC criminality, as the headquarters and subunits of these specific corporations often operate in complete different environments. This thesis recommends further empirical research in other cases of PMSC involvement in international crimes to substantiate the explanatory power of subunits and a bidirectional approach. In addition, even though subunit analysis and a bidirectional approach may find some ground in explaining the opportunity structure and (lack of) social control mechanisms for the creation of crimes within PMSCs, it is not sufficient in explaining the motivation of the perpetrators. In order to explain why the crimes are committed in the first place, more research must be done on the motivation of PMSCs from a perpetrator's perspective in both the home state and within the subunits of the host state.

References

Adhikari v. Daoud & Partners. (2014). 994 F.Supp.2d 831 (U.S. District Court, S.D. Texas).

Albanese, J. S. (1982a). *Organizational offenders: Why solutions fail to political, corporate, and organized crime*. Niagara Falls, NY: Apocalypse.

Albanese, J. S. (1982b). What lockheed and la cosa nostra have in common: The effect of ideology on criminal justice policy. *Crime and Delinquency, 28*, 211–232.

Aronson, E. (2004). *The social animal*. New York: Worth Publishers.

Bandura, A. (1999). Moral disengagement in the perpetration of inhumanities. *Personality and Social Psychology Review, 3*, 193–209.

Barnett, H. C. (1981). Corporate capitalism, corporate crime. *Crime and Delinquency, 27*(1), 4–23.

Baum, J. A., & McGahan, A. M. (2009). *Outsourcing war: The evolution of the private military industry after the Cold War*. Available at SSRN: https://ssrn.com/abstract=1496498

Blaustein, J. (2012). *Policy translations for police reform in Bosnia and Herzegovina*. Master's thesis, University of Edinburgh, Edinburgh.

Bolkovac, K., & Lynn, C. (2011). *The whistleblower: Sex trafficking, military contractors, and one woman's fight for justice*. New York: Palgrave Macmillan.

Box, S. (1983). *Ideology, crime and mystification*. London: Tavistock.

Braithwaite, J. (1985). White collar crime. *Annual Review of Sociology, 11*, 1–25.

Braithwaite, J. (1989). Criminological theory and organizational crime. *Justice Quarterly, 6*, 333–358.

Brown, A. K. (2007). Baghdad bound: Forced labor of third-country nationals in Iraq. *Rutgers Law Review, 60*, 737–767.

Cameron, L. (2006). Private military companies: Their status under international humanitarian law and its impact on their regulation. *International Review of the Red Cross, 88*(863), 573–598.

Chambliss, W. J. (1988). *On the take: From petty crooks to presidents*. Bloomington: Indiana University Press.

Chambliss, W. J. (1989). State-organized crime. *Criminology, 27*, 183–208.

Chatterjee, P. (2010). *Halliburton's army: How a well-connected Texas oil company revolutionized the way America makes war*. New York: Nation Books.

Clinard, M. (1946). Criminological theories of violations of wartime regulations. *American Sociological Review, 11*, 258–270.

Clinard, M., & Yeager, P. (1980). *Corporate crime: The first comprehensive account of illegal practices among America's top corporations*. New York: Free Press.

Cohen, D. V. (1995). Ethics and crime in business firms: Organizational culture and the impact of anomie. *Advances in Criminological Theory, 6*, 183–206.

Coleman, J. W. (1987). Toward an integrated theory of white-collar crime. *American Journal of Sociology, 93*, 406–439.

© The Author(s) 2018

C. Cole, R. Vermeltfoort, *U.S. Government Contractors and Human Trafficking*, SpringerBriefs in Criminology, https://doi.org/10.1007/978-3-319-70827-0

Cressey, D. R. (1950). The criminal violation of financial trust. *American Sociological Review, 15*, 738–743.
Cutler, C. (2010). The legitimacy of private transnational governance: Experts and the transnational market for force. *Socio-Economic Review, 8*, 157–185.
Djelic, M., & Sahlin-Andersson, K. (Eds.). (2006). *Transnational governance*. Cambridge: Cambridge University Press.
Ermann, M. D., & Lundman, R. J. (1978). *Corporate and governmental deviance: Problems of organizational behavior in contemporary society*. New York: Oxford University Press.
Festinger, L. (1957). *A theory of cognitive dissonance*. Stanford: Stanford University Press.
Festinger, L., & Carlsmith, J. M. (1959). Cognitive consequences of forced compliance. *Journal of Abnormal and Social Psychology, 58*, 203–210.
Filartiga v. Pena-Irala. (1980). U.S. App. LEXIS 16111 (U.S. 2d Cir. 1980).
Finney, H. C., & Lesieur, H. R. (1982). A contingency theory of organizational crime. *Research in the Sociology of Organizations, 1*, 255–299.
Flood, M. (2008). Men, sex, and homosociality: How bonds between men shape their sexual relations with women. *Men and Masculinities, 10*(3), 339–359.
George, A. L., & Bennett, A. (2005). *Case studies and theory development in the social sciences*. Cambridge: MIT Press.
Gibson, J. T. (1990). Factors contributing to the creation of a torturer. In P. Suedfeld (Ed.), *Psychology and torture* (pp. 77–88). New York: Hemisphere.
Gottfredson, M. R., & Hirschi, T. (1990). *A general theory of crime*. Stanford: Stanford University Press.
Gross, E. (1978). Organizational crime: A theoretical perspective. In N. K. Denzin (Ed.), *Studies in symbolic interaction* (Vol. 1, pp. 55–85). Greenwich, CT: JAI Press.
Hays, P.A. (2004). Case study research. In: de Marrais, K. & Lapan, S.D. (Eds.), Foundations for research: Methods of inquiry in education and the social sciences. 217–234). London: Lawrence Erlbaum.
Hirschi, T., & Gottfredson, M. (1987). Causes of white-collar crime. *Criminology, 25*, 949–974.
Hirschi, T., & Gottfredson, M. (1989). The significance of white-collar crime for a general theory of crime. *Criminology, 27*, 359–371.
Hopkins, A. (1978). The anatomy of corporate crime. In P. R. Wilson & J. Braithwaite (Eds.), *Two faces of deviance: Crimes of the powerless and powerful* (pp. 79–91). Brisbane, QLD: University of Queensland Press.
Huisman, W. (2008). Corporations and international crimes. In A. Smeulers & R. Haveman (Eds.), *Supranational criminology. Towards a criminology of international crimes* (pp. 181–211). Antwerpen: Intersentia.
Huisman, W. (2010). *Business as usual? Corporate involvement in international crimes*. The Hague: Eleven International.
Isenberg, D. (2009). *Shadow force: Private security contractors in Iraq*. Santa Barbara, CA: ABC-CLIO.
John Doe I et al. v. UNOCAL Corp. et al. (2002). 395 F.3d 932 (U.S. 9th Cir. 2002).
Kaptein, M. (2004). Business codes of multinational firms: What do they say? *Journal of Business Ethics, 50*, 13–31.
Kaptein, M., & Wempe, J. (2002). *The balanced company: A theory of corporate integrity*. Oxford: Oxford University Press.
Kaptein, M., Klamer, H., & Wierenga, A. (2003). *De bedrijfscode: Aanleiding, inhoud, invoering en effectiviteit*. Den Haag: NCW, Ethicon, Stichting Beroepsmoraal en Misdaadpreventie.
Kauzlarich, D., & Kramer, R. C. (1998a). *Crimes of the American nuclear state: At home and abroad*. Lebanon, NH: University Press of New England.
Kauzlarich, D., & Kramer, R. C. (1998b). Explaining and controlling the crimes of the nuclear state. In D. Kauzlarich & R. C. Kramer (Eds.), *Crimes of the American nuclear state: At home and abroad*. Lebanon, NH: University Press of New England.

Kelman, H. C. (2005). The policy context of torture: A social-psychological analysis. *International Review of the Red Cross, 87*, 123–134.
Kiobel v. Royal Dutch Petroleum Co. (2013). 133 S.Ct. 1659 (U.S. Supreme Court 2013).
Kramer, R. C. (1990a). *From white-collar crime to state-corporate crime*. Paper presented at the North Central Sociological Association.
Kramer, R. C. (1990b). *State-corporate crime*. Paper presented at the North Central sociological Association and the Southern Sociological Association, Louisville, KY.
Kramer, R. C., & Michalowski, R. J. (1990, November). *Toward an integrated theory of state-corporate crime*. Paper presented at a meeting of the American Society of Criminology, Baltimore, MD.
Kramer, R. C., & Michalowski, R. J. (1993). *State-corporate crime: Case studies in organizational deviance*. Unpublished manuscript.
Kramer, R. C., Michalowski, R. J., & Kauzlarich, D. (2002). The origins and development of the concept and theory of state-corporate crime. *Crime and Delinquency, 48*(2), 263–282.
Kramer, R. C., & Michalowski, R. J. (2006). The original formulation. In R. J. Michalowski & R. C. Kramer (Eds.), *State-corporate crime: Wrongdoing at the intersection of business and government* (pp. 18–26). New Brunswick, NJ: Rutgers University Press.
Lane, R. E. (1953). Why businessmen violate the law. *Criminal Law Journal, 44*, 151–415.
Lehnardt, C. (2007). *Private military companies and state responsibility*. Oxford, England: Oxford University Press.
Li, D. (2015). Offshoring the army: Migrant workers and the US military. *UCLA Law Review, 62*, 123–174.
Maffai, M. (2008). Accountability for private military and security company employees that engage in sex trafficking and related abuses while under contract with the United States overseas. *Wisconsin International Law Journal, 26*(4), 1095–1139.
Mattar, M. Y. (2011). Interpreting judicial interpretations of the criminal statutes of the trafficking victims protection act: Ten years later. *American University Journal of Gender Social Policy and Law, 19*(4), 1247–1304.
Matza, D., & Sykes, G. M. (1957). Techniques of neutralization. A theory of delinquency. *American Journal of Sociology, 22*, 664–670.
Mendelson, S. E. (2005). *Barracks and brothels: Peacekeepers and human trafficking in the Balkans*. Washington, DC: CSIS Press.
Messerschmidt, J. W. (1986). *Capitalism, patriarchy, and crime: Toward a socialist feminist criminology*. Totowa, NJ: Roman and Littlefield.
Michalowski, R. J. (1985). *Order, law, and crime – An introduction to criminology*. Westminister, MD: Random House Distribution Center.
Michalowski, R. J., & Kramer, R. C. (1987). The space between laws: The problem of corporate crime in a transnational context. *Social Problems, 34*, 34–53.
Mills, C. W. (1956). *The power elite*. New York: Oxford University Press.
Murray, J. (2003). Who will police the peace-builders? The failure to establish accountability for the participation of United Nations Civilian Police in the trafficking of women in post-conflict Bosnia and Herzegovina. *Columbia Human Rights Law Review, 34*, 475–527.
Obokata, T. (2005). Trafficking of human beings as a crime against humanity: Some implications for the international legal system. *International and Comparative Law Quarterly, 54*(2), 445–458.
Offe, C., & Ronge, V. (1982). Theses on the theory of the state. In A. Giddens & D. Held (Eds.), *Classes, power and conflict* (pp. 249–256). Berkeley, CA: University of California Press.
Ortiz, C. (2004). Regulating private military companies: States and the expanding business of commercial security provision. In K. van der Pijl, L. Assassi, & D. Wigan (Eds.), *Global regulation. Managing crises after the imperial turn* (pp. 205–219). Basingstoke, UK: Palgrave Macmillan.
Passas, N. (1990). Anomie and corporate deviance. *Contemporary Crises, 14*, 157–178.
Perrow, C. (1961). The analysis of goals in complex organizations. *American Sociological Review, 26*, 854–866.

Pugliese, E. (2007). Organ trafficking and the TVPA: Why one word makes a difference in international enforcement efforts. *Journal of Contemporary Health Law and Policy, 24*(1), 181–208.
Radovanovic, M., & Kartusch, A. (2001). *Report on the combat of trafficking in women for the purpose of forced prostitution in Bosnia and Herzegovina*. Vienna: Ludwig Boltzman Institute of Human Rights.
Reid v. Covert. (1956). 354 U.S. 1 (U.S. Supreme Court, 1956).
Rothe, D. L. (2006). Iraq and Halliburton. In R. J. Michalowski & R. C. Kramer (Eds.), *State-corporate crime: Wrongdoing at the intersection of business and government* (pp. 215–238). New Brunswick, NJ: Rutgers University Press.
Rothe, D. L., & Ross, I. R. (2010). Private military contractors, crime, and the terrain of unaccountability. *Justice Quarterly, 27*, 593–617.
Rothe, D. L., & Mullins, C. W. (2011). *State crime: Current perspectives*. New York: Rutgers University Press.
Ryngaert, C. (2008). Litigating abuses committed by private military companies. *The European Journal of International Law, 19*, 1035–1053.
Schiff, B. N. (2008). *Building the International Criminal Court*. Cambridge: Cambridge University Press.
Schrager, L. S., & Short, J. F. (1978). Toward a sociology of organizational crime. *Social Problems, 25*, 407–419.
Scully, D. (1990). *Understanding sexual violence: A study of convicted rapists*. Boston: Unwin Hyman.
Singer, P. W. (2001). Corporate warriors: The rise of the privatized military industry and its ramifications for international security. *International Security, 26*(3), 186–220.
Singer, P. W. (2011). *Corporate warriors: The rise of the privatized military industry*. Ithaca, NY: Cornell University Press.
Sklansky, D. A. (1998). The private police. *UCLA Law Review, 46*, 1165–1287.
Sklar, M. J. (1988). *The corporate reconstruction of American capitalism, 1890–1916: The market, the law, and politics*. Cambridge, UK: Cambridge University Press.
Smeulers, A., & Grünfeld, F. (2011). *International crimes and other gross human rights violations*. Leiden: Martinus Nijhoff.
Soons, D. (2011). *CACI and Titan in Iraq*. Unpublished master's thesis, Vrije Universiteit Amsterdam, Amsterdam, NL.
Sriram, C. L., Martin-Ortega, O., & Herman, J. (2014). *War, conflict and human rights: Theory and practice*. London: Routledge.
Stone, D. (1975). *Where the law ends: The social control of corporate behavior*. New York: Harper and Row.
Sutherland, E. H. (1940). White collar criminality: Presidential address to the American society of sociology. *American Sociological Review, 5*, 1–12.
Sutherland, E. H. (1949). *White collar crime*. New York: Holt, Rinehart and Winston.
Sutherland, E. H. (1956). Crime of corporations. In A. Cohen, A. Lindesmith, & K. Schuessler (Eds.), *The Sutherland papers*. Bloomington, IN: Indiana University Press.
Tyler, C. N. (2012). Limitations of the contingency contracting framework: Finding effective ways to police foreign subcontractors in Iraq and Afghanistan. *Public Contract Law Journal, 41*(2), 453–472.
Vaughan, D. (1982). Toward understanding unlawful organizational behavior. *Michigan Law Review, 80*, 1377–1402.
Vaughan, D. (1983). *Controlling unlawful organizational behavior: Social structure and corporate misconduct*. Chicago: University of Chicago Press.
Waits, K. E. (2006). Avoiding the legal Bermuda Triangle: The Military Extraterritorial Jurisdiction Act's unprecedented expansion of US criminal jurisdiction over foreign nationals. *Arizona Journal of International and Comparative Law, 23*(2), 493–498.
White, M. D., & Terry, K. J. (2008). Child sexual abuse in the Catholic Church revisiting the rotten apples explanation. *Criminal Justice and Behavior, 35*(5), 658–678.

Yin, R. (1994). *Case study research: Design and methods*. Beverly Hills, CA: Sage.
Young, T. R. (1981). Corporate crime: A critique of the Clinard report. *Crime, Law and Social Change, 5*(3), 323–336.

Interviews

Interview 1: Kathryn Bolkovac, former DynCorp employee. Worked for DynCorp during the UNMBIH in BiH (London, 11 June 2014).
Interview 2: Madeleine Rees, Head of the UN Office of the High Commissionaire for Human Rights during the UNMBIH in BiH (London, 12 June 2014).

Internet

Adviesraad Internationale Vraagstukken (AIV). (2007). *De inhuur van private militaire bedrijven: Een kwestie van verantwoordelijkheid*. The Hague: AIV.
Al Jazeera. (2014, March 12). America's war workers. *Al Jazeera*. Retrieved June 17, 2016, from http://www.aljazeera.com/programmes/faultlines/2014/03/america-war-workers-201431112381160 9515.html
American Civil Liberties Union (ACLU), & Yale Law School International Human Rights Clinic. (2012). *Victims of complacency – The ongoing trafficking and abuse of third country nationals by U.S. government contractors*. Retrieved June 17, 2016, from https://www.aclu.org/files/assets/hrp_traffickingreport_web_0.pdf
Ashton, A. (2008, December 2). Military contractor in Iraq holds foreign workers in warehouses. *McClathy Newspapers*. Retrieved June 17, 2016, from http://www.mcclatchydc.com/news/nation-world/world/article24512842.html
Aston, J. N., & Paranjape, V. N. (2012). *Human trafficking and its prosecution: Challenges of the ICC*. Symbiosis Law School, Pune. Retrieved June 17, 2016, from http://www.peacepalacelibrary.nl/ebooks/files/356626199.pdf
Bauman, R. H., Reid, R. H., & Mc Dermid, C. (2011, March 16). Contractors watching contractors? Where is the true oversight? (part I). *truthout.org*. Retrieved June 17, 2016, from http://truth-out.org/archive/component/k2/item/94942:contractors-watching-contractors-where-is-the-true-oversight-part-i
BBC News. (2007, October 30). Iraq to end contractor immunity. *BBC News*. Retrieved June 17, 2016, from http://news.bbc.co.uk/2/hi/middle_east/7069173.stm
Coalition Provisional Authority. (2004). *Order Number 17 – Status of the Coalition Provisional Authority, MNF – Iraq, Certain missions and personnel in Iraq*. Retrieved June 17, 2016, from http://www.iraqcoalition.org/regulations/20040627_CPAORD_17_Status_of_Coalition__Rev__with_Annex_A.pdf
CorpWatch. (2002, January 14). *US: DynCorp Disgrace*. Consulted on: http://www.corpwatch.org/article.php?id=11119
Davies, C. (2011, February 28). Briton Danny Fitzsimons jailed in Iraq for contractors' murders. *The Guardian*. Retrieved June 17, 2016, from https://www.theguardian.com/world/2011/feb/28/danny-fitzsimons-jailed-iraq-murders
Dayton Peace Agreement. (1995, November 21). *General framework agreement for peace in Bosnia and Herzegovinia*. Consulted on: http://www.refworld.org/docid/3de495c34.html
DynCorp International. (2012). *Codes of ethics and business conduct*. Virginia: DI. Consulted on: http://www.dyn-intl.com/media/coe_bc_brochure.pdf

Employment Tribunals (2002). Bolkovac v. DynCorp Aerospace Operations (UK) Ltd. "*Unanimous Decision*." Case no. 3102729/01. Consulted on: http://www.contractormisconduct.org/ass/contractors/59/cases/688/765/veritas-capital-dyncorp-in-bosnia_bolkovac-decision.pdf

Gillison, D. (2014, January 17). U.S. contractor KBR sees Iraq human trafficking, execution case tossed. *100 reporters – New journalism for a new age*. Retrieved June 17, 2016, from https://100r.org/2014/01/u-s-contractor-kbr-sees-iraq-human-trafficking-execution-case-tossed/

Goldberg, M. (2011, June 29). Today's hidden slave trade. *The Daily Beast*. Retrieved June 17, 2016, from http://www.thedailybeast.com/articles/2011/06/28/world-s-hidden-slave-trade-includes-forced-labor-in-u-s-military-contracting.html

Human Rights Watch. (2002). *Hopes betrayed: Trafficking of women and girls to post-war Bosnia and Herzegovina for forced prostitution*. New York: Human Rights Watch.

Information Memorandum to the State Department. (2000). *Subject: Trafficking in women in Bosnia – Recent events*. Consulted on: http://www.contractormisconduct.org/ass/contractors/59/cases/688/767/veritas-capital-dyncorp-in-bosnia_state-dept-memo.pdf

International Labor Organization. (1930). *Convention concerning forced or compulsory labor (No. 29)*. Retrieved June 17, 2016, from http://www.ilo.org/dyn/normlex/en/f?p=NORMLEXPUB:12100:0::NO::P12100_ILO_CODE:C029

International Labor Organization. (2012). *ILO indicators of forced labor*. Retrieved June 17, 2016, from http://www.ilo.org/wcmsp5/groups/public/---ed_norm/---declaration/documents/publication/wcms_203832.pdf

International Labor Organization. (2014). *The meanings of forced labor*. Retrieved June17, 2016, from http://www.ilo.org/global/topics/forced-labour/news/WCMS_237569/lang--en/index.htm

Investopedia. (n.d.). *Cost-plus contract*. Retrieved June 17, 2016, from http://www.investopedia.com/terms/c/cost-plus-contract.asp

IPOA. (2006). *State of the Peace and Stability Operations Industry Survey 2006*. Consulted on: http://ipoaonline.org/php/index.php?option=com_content&task=view&id=103&Itemid=110

Isenberg, D. (2012, August 16). The invisible foreign subcontractor. *The Huffington Post*. Retrieved June 17, 2016, from http://www.huffingtonpost.com/david-isenberg/the-invisible-foreign-sub_b_1785420.html

Isenberg, D., & Schwellenbach, N. (2011, June 14). Documents reveal details of alleged labor trafficking by KBR subcontractor. *Project on Government Oversight*. Retrieved June 17, 2016, from http://www.pogo.org/our-work/articles/2011/co-ht-20110614.html

James, B. (2002). *Firing of former officer unfair, court rules: Whistleblower upheld in UN Bosnia police case*. Consulted on: http://www.nytimes.com/2002/08/08/news/08iht-un_ed3_.html

Kavinnamannil, S., & McCahon, S. (2011, May). In the name of progress – Illegal human labor trafficking within government contracts. *Fraud Magazine*. Retrieved June 17, 2016, from http://www.fraud-magazine.com/article.aspx?id=4294969377

Lilia Diu, N. (2012). *What the UN doesn't want you to know*. Consulted on: http://www.telegraph.co.uk/culture/film/9041974/What-the-UN-Doesnt-Want-You-to-Know.html

Moyer, R. M. (2011). *Soldiers for hire: The role of private military contractors in Iraq*. Retrieved June 17, 2016, from http://www.anselm.edu/Documents/NHIOP/Global%20Topics/Archive/Moyerfinal09.pdf

Peters, H. M., Schwartz, M., & Kapp, L. (2015). *Department of defense contractor and troop levels in Iraq and Afghanistan: 2007–2015*. Congressional Research Service (CRS). Retrieved June 17, 2016, from https://www.fas.org/sgp/crs/natsec/R44116.pdf

Picarelli, J. T. (2002). *Trafficking, slavery and peacekeeping: The need for a comprehensive training program*. Consulted on: http://traccc.gmu.edu/pdfs/publications/human_traffickingpublications/TIP&PKO_EWG_Report_Final.pdf

Rohde, D. L. (2004, May 2). The struggle for Iraq: Foreign labor: Indians who worked in Iraq complain of exploitation. *International New York Times*. Retrieved June 17, 2016, from http://www.nytimes.com/2004/05/07/world/struggle-for-iraq-foreign-labor-indians-who-worked-iraq-complain-exploitation.html?_r=0

Schwartz, M., & Swain, J. (2011). *Department of Defense contractors in Afghanistan and Iraq: Background and analysis*. Congressional Research Service (CRS). Retrieved June 17, 2016, from https://www.fas.org/sgp/crs/natsec/R40764.pdf

Schwartz, M., & Church, J. (2013). *Department of Defense's use of contractors to support military operations: Background, analysis, and issues for Congress*. Congressional Research Service (CRS). Retrieved June 17, 2016, from https://www.fas.org/sgp/crs/natsec/R43074.pdf

Simic, O. (2004). *Accountability of UN civilian police involved in trafficking of women in Bosnia and Herzegovina*. Consulted on: http://www.monitor.upeace.org/innerpg.cfm?id_article=219

Singer, P. W. (2004). *The private military industry and Iraq: What have we learned and where to next?* Geneva Centre for the Democratic Control of Armed Forces – Policy Paper. Retrieved June 17, 2016, from http://www.dcaf.ch/Publications/The-Private-Military-Industry-and-Iraq

Singer, P. W. (2007). *Can't win with'em, can't go to war without'em: Private military contractors and counterinsurgency*. Brookings Institution Washington, DC – Foreign Policy Paper Series. Retrieved June 17, 2016, from http://www.brookings.edu/research/papers/2007/09/27militarycontractors and http://www.brookings.edu/~/media/research/files/papers/2007/9/27militarycontractors/0927militarycontractors.pdf

Simpson, C. (2005, October 9). Iraq: Desperate for work, lured into danger. *The Chicago Tribune*. Retrieved June 17, 2016, from http://articles.chicagotribune.com/2005-10-09/news/0510090434_1_iraq-restaurant-middle-east

Smallteacher, R. (2014, January 17). Trafficking lawsuit against KBR for wrongful deaths in Iraq dismissed. *CorpWatch – Holding Corporations Accountable*. Retrieved June 17, 2016, from http://www.corpwatch.org/article.php?id=15921

Stiglmayer, A. (2011). *Sexual violence: Systematic rape*. Consulted on: http://www.crimesofwar.org/a-z-guide/sexual-violence-systematic-rape/

Stillman, S. (2011a, June 6). The invisible army. *The New Yorker*. Retrieved June 17, 2016, from http://www.newyorker.com/magazine/2011/06/06/the-invisible-army

Stillman, S. (2011b, June 7). The dancing cowboy whistleblower. *The New Yorker*. Retrieved June 17, 2016, from http://www.newyorker.com/news/news-desk/the-dancing-cowboy-whistleblower

Tavernise, S. (2008, July 2). U.S. agrees to lift immunity for contractors in Iraq. *The New York Times*. Retrieved June 17, 2016, from http://www.nytimes.com/2008/07/02/world/middleeast/02iraq.html

Trafficking Victims Protection Reauthorization Act (TVPRA). (2005). Retrieved June 17, 2016, from http://www.state.gov/j/tip/laws/61106.htm

Trafficking Victims Protection Reauthorization Act (TVPRA). (2008). Retrieved June 17, 2016, from http://www.state.gov/j/tip/laws/113178.htm

United Nations Office on Drugs and Crime. (2016). *What is human trafficking?* Retrieved June 17, 2016, from https://www.unodc.org/unodc/en/human-trafficking/what-is-human-trafficking.html

United Nations Organization. (2000). *United Nations protocol to prevent, suppress and punish trafficking in persons*. Retrieved June 17, 2016, from http://www.osce.org/odihr/19223?download=true

United States Council for International Business (USCIB). (2007). *Issue Analysis – U.S. ratification of core ILO labor standards*. Retrieved June 17, 2016, from https://www.uscib.org/docs/US_Ratification_of_ILO_Core_Conventions.pdf

United States Department of Defense (DoD). (2014). *Strategic plan for combating trafficking in persons (CTIP) 2014-2018*. Retrieved June 17, 2016, from http://ctip.defense.gov/Portals/12/Documents/Strategic_Plan_FINAL.pdf

Women's International League for Peace and Freedom. (2013). *Project paths to justice*. Consulted on: http://www.wilpfinternational.org/paths-to-justice/

Young, A. (2013, March 19). And the winner for the most Iraq war contracts is … KBR, with $39.5 billion in a decade. *International Business Times*. Retrieved June 17, 2016, from http://www.ibtimes.com/winner-most-iraq-war-contracts-kbr-395-billion-decade-1135905

Index

© The Author(s) 2018

C. Cole, R. Vermeltfoort, *U.S. Government Contractors and Human Trafficking*, SpringerBriefs in Criminology, https://doi.org/10.1007/978-3-319-70827-0

FSC
www.fsc.org
MIX
Papier | Fördert gute Waldnutzung
FSC® C083411

Kolibri 360 GmbH
Ferdinand-Jühlke-Straße 7
99095 Erfurt, Deutschland
produktsicherheit@kolibri360.de